Working with Anthroposophy

By the same author:

Stages of Consciousness (1984)
Becoming Aware of the Logos (1985)
From Normal to Healthy (1988)
The Life of the Soul (1990)

Working with Anthropósophy

Georg Kühlewind

Translated by Michael Lipson and Christopher Bamford

ANTHROPOSOPHIC PRESS

This book is a translation of *Vom Umgang mit der Anthroposophie* published by Verlag Freies Geistesleben, GmbH Stuttgart, 1991, with additions by the author.

Published by permission of the author.

Published by Anthroposophic Press, Inc.

Library of Congress Cataloging-in-Publication Data

Kühlewind, Georg.
[Vom Umgang mit der Anthroposophie. English]
Working with Anthroposophy / Georg Kühlewind ; with an introduction by Jörgen Smit ; translated by Michael Lipson and Christopher Bamford.
Translation of: Vom Umgang mit der Anthroposophie.
ISBN 0-88010-361-2
I. Title.
BP595.K78813 1991
299'.935–dc20 91-41360
CIP

Texts by Rudolf Steiner printed in the Appendices are translated by permission of Rudolf Steiner Nachlassverwaltung, Dornach, Switzerland. They are published in German by Rudolf Steiner Verlag, Dornach, Switzerland.

Printed in the United States of America

Contents

Foreword 7

Introduction 11

1. The Character of Spiritual Science 17
2. Healthy Human Understanding 21
3. Contents 23
4. Knowledge and Ability: Knowing and Doing 25
5. Enslavement 28
6. Temptation 31
7. Right Study 35

AFTERWORD

1. The Transmission of Anthroposophy 39
2. On Speculative Anthroposophy 43

APPENDICES

I. Understanding Imagistic Descriptions 49

II. Deductive Reason and the Supersensible 50

III. Remembering Contents and the "State of the Soul" 51

IV. Healthy Human Understanding 52

V. Pure Thinking 59

VI. Mantras: Their Origin and Practice 60

VII. Enthusiasm and Mysticism 63

VIII. "Explanation" of "Contents" 64

IX. Temptation 66

X. New Concepts 70
XI. First Steps 75
XII. Study as the Way to Pure Thinking 77
XIII. Active, Clairvoyant Thinking 79
XIV. The Experience of Thinking 80
XV. Wordless Thinking 80
XVI. The "Two Ways" 83
XVII. Building Community 84
XVIII. Scientificality 85
XIX. The Cultivation of Spiritual Science 85
XX. Understanding Spiritual Truths 87

Notes 89
References 91

Foreword

Because of the way in which Rudolf Steiner presents spiritual facts, readers or listeners meeting anthroposophy for the first time frequently experience a spontaneous feeling of its obviousness arising within them.

They know with certainty, "This is undoubtedly so," or "I actually already knew this, but now it is clear to me and I am consciously aware of it," or "I have definitely experienced this before."

Such an insight may have to do with a basic characteristic of human nature. Very often it is related to the laws of biography. A person has experienced or suffered a fact and now this fact is clearly and convincingly understood. Perhaps there is a description of repeated earth lives and suddenly, without intention or meditative practice, vivid images of life in other times rise up that can hardly be anything but pictures of some past life on earth and that are immediately interpreted as such. Or, in the midst of a description by Rudolf Steiner, a person suddenly experiences — coming from apparently distant, high spheres of the spiritual worlds — the complete disappearance of his or her physical surroundings and the convincing and obvious "presence" of the spiritual reality described.

What is going on here? Unconsciously, present-day human beings have reached the threshold of the spiritual world. Often only the slightest impulse from without will allow spiritual facts somehow to penetrate into consciousness. The human etheric body is slowly beginning to loosen and free itself from bondage to the physical body and, without prior schooling in thinking or meditation, spontaneous clairvoyant experiences occur.

In this situation a boundary zone forms before, on, and beyond the threshold of the spiritual world. The possibility of delusion in this zone is very great. For just as our cognitive activity completes every physical-sensory perception, as it were by bringing it "up" to true reality, so every supersensible perception of spiritual facts needs as it were to be brought "down" by our thinking-cognizing activity. Only if this happens can true reality be grasped.

In this boundary zone surrounding the threshold of the spiritual world, it is only too easy for ideas that have not been worked through in thinking – half-conscious remains of memories, unpenetrated wishes, drives and desires – to mix with the experience of spiritual facts. And all too often delusion and superstition result.

Thus this zone, in which modern humanity consciously, semiconsciously, or quite unconsciously, seeks longingly for its true being in the spiritual world, requires as a precondition for the search for truth a radical cleansing or catharsis: one that can be achieved only by thorough self-knowledge, a change of life, and a purifying schooling of thinking.

This situation is compounded by the ever increasing inflation of words by all the mass media and by the flood of printed texts. Where does the torrent of words end and thinking begin? The inflation of words does not, of course, stop at the doors of the Anthroposophical Society. The activity of thinking – independent of words – must always be practiced anew with inner effort, so that out of this purely spiritual power each word can be filled anew, from within, with facts grasped in thinking.

This purification is a particular concern of Georg Kühlewind whose works repeatedly draw attention to the importance of a vigorous schooling of thinking as the precondition of the path to truth. In *Working with Anthroposophy*, he approaches the question of how to study anthroposophy and how to work with Rudolf Steiner's spiritual science.

Particularly striking passages relating to this theme have been gathered from Steiner's work in the Appendices. Here, from various angles, the cleansing of the boundary zone—the overcoming of the sources of deception at the threshold of the spiritual world—is characterized in stern language.

This work of purifying cognition by a schooling of thinking has an added, special significance at the present moment when, in the immediate vicinity of the Anthroposophical Society, a special "flora" of some thirty different "occult" movements has sprung up—into which anthroposophists repeatedly fall, obviously because they have insufficiently practiced the faculty of discernment in this border zone at the threshold of the spiritual world.

A thorough cleansing along these lines would seem to be relevant. May this book contribute to it.

JÖRGEN SMIT

Dornach, November 1990

Introduction

Anthropsophy appeals to thinking as an idea and, through thinking, it can speak to the heart as a luminous warmth. For about a hundred and fifty years a battle has waged continuously around the question of thinking. The issue is, Will thinking succumb to the mechanism of the brain? Will "the brain thinks" become reality? Or will thinking strengthen itself in its autonomy, and thereby become able to think actively, freely, and even oppose the existing mechanisms of the brain, dissolving and transforming them? When the cerebral apparatus dominates thinking, it makes no difference *what* we think, or think we think.

Anthroposophy, for its part, presupposes that thinking does not remain bound to the brain, its instrument. It recognizes that when thinking is determined by the brain it loses its autonomy and can no longer act freely – in which case the assumption that the brain thinks becomes a reality.

Working with anthroposophy can help make our thinking and psychological being ever more independent of the predetermined structures of the brain and the physical body. The aim of studying anthroposophy, therefore, is not knowledge of some contents falsely considered as information but is an activity, an event. This aim would be completely illusory, however, were we not to some extent already *touching* superconscious planes of consciousness from moment to moment in our everyday lives with *each new understanding.*

At the level of study, the goal of working with anthroposophy is to extend this "touching," and thereby increase the experience of these insight-flashes. *Metanoia* or "change of mind" means that *practicing* readers – those who exercise or meditate – transform not only the contents but the *level* of their consciousness. The contents serve this goal because their real meaning is revealed only to heightened consciousness. One reads much more slowly when seeking the *how* of what is presented (see Appendix XV) and not simply its "contents." Study, therefore, in this context means reading and exercising (meditating).

Working with Anthroposophy has two goals: to stimulate both meditative working with spiritual science and new, independent formulations of its content on the basis of experience. For times are changing quickly, much more quickly than before. The founder of spiritual science knew this perfectly well.

Truths cannot be transmitted simply as stable dogmas. Truths are always of a given moment and at each moment must be grasped anew. This demands at each moment a renewed activity in relation to the human gift of understanding (See Appendix XX).

One way of working with anthroposophy is presented and recommended here – a way appropriate for today, and perhaps for tomorrow as well. This does not mean that the author despises or condemns other ways of working with anthroposophy. On the contrary, he bows down spiritually before those who have transmitted anthroposophy to him in their very different way, and also before those who, in the future, will develop further methods quite different from his own. It is his hope that this will take place — for a teaching lives only as long as it grows and changes.

"The development that spiritual science carries out in us is far more important than the content of spiritual science."[1].

Working with anthroposophy should not lead to evading anthroposophy.

Working with Anthroposophy

1.

The Character of Spiritual Science

ALL SCIENCES, except spiritual science, work on the same level of consciousness. This level of consciousness is characterized by the fact that it contains and consists of the products or results of processes, while the processes that gave rise to these products or results generally remain unnoticed and unexperienced. Such is the case, for example, with the thinking that produces thoughts, for a thought, after all, is the finished product of the thinking process. To be understood, such a finished thought—expressed acoustically or in written form—must become momentarily alive again and fluid in a new thinking, a second process of thinking.

Typically we do not notice, or only barely experience, this melting and resolidifying of thought because it takes place so quickly. Familiar thoughts are grasped as thoughts (results, products) by the thought-sense, without any, or with only very little, real thinking.

We may therefore appropriately call this level of consciousness the *informational* level. It consists in statements of information such as "this is how it is," or "this is how it works." Statements of this kind underlie the questions asked by the natural sciences (and the other sciences constructed in imitation of the scientific method)—questions like "Why?" "What is it made of?" and "How?" Such questions are all analytic. What is being analyzed, however, has always been *given* as a unity by previous knowledge or insight—either consciously or, if it dates from childhood, unconsciously.

Ultimately, such knowledge or insight can be traced back to elements that became conscious without mediation—for example, to the first words, concepts, sense-qualities, etc., that were understood.

If, on the other hand, instead of understanding information, we want to understand a text, then we have to ask a different question. We must ask, "What does that *mean*?" We do not ask what the signs, for instance, or the letters, are made of, or why they follow one another in a given way, or how they came onto the paper, what shape they have, or how far they are from one another. We can read and understand a text only from above: we must leave behind the literal level of the individual letters in order to reach the words; and, likewise, we have to leave behind the level of the words so as to reach the *meaning* of the sentence. It is in the reading, understanding consciousness that meaning *arises*. Meaning is not a thing: it is identical neither with any of the signs that express it in the perceptual world, nor with their totality. In the same way, any phenomenon—including cognition—can be understood only from above.

Spiritual science is directed precisely to the realm (the processes) from which the other sciences draw their contents. The world-picture of everyday consciousness, whose level is the same as that of science, is likewise built up from this realm. Its world is the world of knowing and the knower, and not the world of the known in the normal sense. The *meaning* of a sentence is to be found at its lowest level; from there it reaches upward to ever higher levels of consciousness. Spiritual science, therefore, should be neither pursued nor understood on the informational level. To rise from this level to a higher one demands constant effort to raise oneself up. Spiritual science is, above all, a *reading* science. The thoughts and pictures that communicate it form the starting points for higher meaning in the same way as letters and words form the starting points for reaching the meaning of a sentence. This kind of reading—whose elements are thoughts, pictures, or percepts—is called *meditating*. Ordinary *understanding*—the flashing forth of a new comprehension—can be considered an instantaneously brief meditation. Meditation is the direct path to *experience* in the realm of spiritual science. Whoever approaches spiritual science in this way can eventually go on to do spiritual scientific research. A preliminary path to understanding the results of such research is thought-intuition. These results are ideas of a higher kind. They can be communicated to the nonmeditating, intuitive thinking—*real* thinking—in two ways.[2]

Every cognition is achieved by means of processes of consciousness and can be dissolved back into them. A cognition, therefore, may be described in terms of such processes. This can also occur with regard to higher cognitions. It is the first of the two ways in which the results of spiritual scientific research may be communicated. The processes of consciousness in higher cognition are, however, unknown at first, and their description is incomprehensible without a certain degree of practice on the path of schooling of consciousness. In the same way, it is nearly impossible to describe the movements of a violinist to someone who has never seen a violin. Nevertheless, the description of processes in consciousness can be so formulated that they cannot be misunderstood: a person will either intuitively discover the reality of what is described, or not.

The second way to communicate the results of supersensible research is pictorially. In this case, pictures replace a perception one cannot have oneself. These pictures, however, must never be taken in the sense of *our* everyday perceptions (and there is great danger of misunderstanding them in this way) for then there arises a representational world on the model of our sense-perceptions—which is then taken for a spiritual world. (See Appendix I) The pictures must be understood and read in their character as symbols, not *interpreted* by everyday understanding. Such pictures can also lead to thought-intuitions, as can sense-perceptions, too, under the right conditions.

The two paths to spiritual science mentioned here are *receptive* gestures; they lead to a certain understanding, but not to the possibility of *living* with the results of spiritual research, of working with them in a free, relevant fashion. When we speculate, combine, or link the results of spiritual research according to reason, we overstep the competence offered by our preliminary understanding. (See Appendix II) Reason works on a lower level than that from which spiritual scientific results originate: to combine dialectical reasoning with the results of intuitive cognition would be to mix—and adulterate—different levels. Nevertheless, there is a great temptation to apply speculatively what has been understood. Since, however, it is not a question of information, any comparison or combination is improper. Even at its lowest level, the spiritual world descends only as far as the plane of *becoming*; "information" about it, therefore, cannot be given in the same way as it can for the world of being. Every attempt to take the results of spiritual research as "contents" leads to their distortion and to countless misunderstandings that veil and conceal the entrance to spiritual science precisely from those who most earnestly seek it. It is the corruption of the teaching.

It should already be clear that knowing and remembering spiritual scientific communications cannot be a primary goal of working with anthroposophy. The aim of spiritual scientific communications is to heighten one's level of consciousness by working with them. (See Appendix III).

2.

Healthy Human Understanding

ONE SOURCE of misunderstandings is certainly to be found in Steiner's very frequent appeal to "healthy, unprejudiced human understanding." Once spiritual truths have been attained through appropriate research and put in proper verbal form, it is said, then they are comprehensible to healthy human understanding. Attention, however, is rarely paid to what Steiner meant by this phrase. If we take account of what he said about it, we would work with his texts far more cautiously. (See Appendix IV)

From the texts cited in Appendix IV, it should be clear that healthy human understanding is by no means something generally given, but rather a great challenge which can hardly be met except through a schooling of consciousness. It is often characterized by Steiner as "pure thinking". This expression is profound; it points to a graduated series of acts of purification with regard to thinking.

The first stage consists in freeing thinking from all emotional admixtures, prejudices, inclinations, and so forth. The second frees it from perceptual elements. Thinking thereby becomes "free of sense-qualities," and yet may still remain abstract, i.e. on the everyday level. (See Appendix V) In the next stage, thinking is cleansed of past-elements. This means that it becomes free of the body and no longer relies on brain processes. It raises itself up to the processual, living, or imaginative plane of *pure, living* thinking. Further higher stages are no longer called "thinking", although they contain living thinking within themselves (cognitive feeling and willing).

Living thinking is healthy, unprejudiced thinking—i.e., "healthy human understanding." It is such living thinking alone that can communicate and understand spiritual research. (See Appendix V)

Whenever one encounters a path or teaching that is to lead to higher cognitions, one has to overcome a paradox. The paradox is that one receives the teaching with an as yet untaught, untransformed consciousness. Such a consciousness actually cannot understand the teachings which surpass its capacities. The ability to find one's way out of this trap (or paradox of consciousness) depends upon two mutually antagonistic gestures. The first is the gesture of modern consciousness—the consciousness soul—which can look at or reflect upon itself, i.e., can move on *two* planes, even if the higher is only fleetingly and seldom touched[3]. The second is a description of the beginning of the path, or of the most accessible part of the teaching, given in such a way that the consciousness striving upward can meet it. This is the path to thought-intuition. If such a meeting of the upward-striving consciousness with the description of the beginning of the path or teaching occurs, then the path is assured from step to step. Only on the path of concrete exercises in consciousness is real understanding of the teaching gradually possible. For provisional or beginning understanding, the consciousness must be raised to the appropriate level of consciousness at least momentarily. Self-reflection can help here, in that it can notice nonunderstanding or inadequate understanding—important experiences for anthroposophical study.

3.

Contents

NAIVE REALISM, the view or deeply rooted attitude that there exist perceptions, thoughts, facts, and so forth *without my participation*—that all these are simply "there"—is perhaps most difficult to overcome in relation to the reading of texts. In fact, however, it is in the area of texts that naive realism could be overcome most quickly and most easily. It is a common, often encountered experience that a text, a book, can tell a reader only what he or she can understand. This is to say that, if I reread the "same" text some time after having first read it, that text can appear quite different to me at this second reading and communicate altogether new contents. From this experience one should easily come to the insight that "contents" only exist for me through my understanding, and that thoughts as thoughts can enter my consciousness only if I allow their dead form—the written or acoustic appearance—to *rise again* within me by *thinking* them. Only through my thinking does a "thought" become accessible to me. Only if I *think* it does a thought become a thought for me (except in the case of long-familiar thoughts, which I can receive through the thought-sense without actually thinking).

Therefore the very widespread view that "spiritual contents" "have an effect" is a result of naive realism, of an epistemologically unschooled naivete. Neither contents nor thoughts exist "in themselves." Like everything else, spiritual contents have intentional reality, i.e., their reality (and therefore also their effectiveness) is determined from two sides: by the author (or thinker) and by the reader (or understander).

Dogmas—contents that are misunderstood or received nominally or inadequately—certainly do have a very definite effect: they allow the life of consciousness to spoil and become diseased. If I receive a "content" in my consciousness without understanding it, or I misunderstand it, or inadequately understand it, and I do not notice this, then this "not-understood content" forms an enclosure, a place where my consciousness no longer circulates properly. My consciousness then becomes diseased: it tends to form further enclosures of this kind within itself. This disease of consciousness necessarily leads to a disease of moral sensitivity—if morality was not already diseased and the disease of cognitive life did not follow precisely from moral sources (for example, from ambition).

The structure of the consciousness of people today makes it impossible for a word to have an immediate effect: a person can decide whether to receive it. This is the basis of human freedom. Demagogues, however, still attempt by their speech to "affect" people's emotional life, not their cognition—which is an attack on human freedom. Likewise, for contemporary consciousness, a "mantric" text is effective only if the text is taken up in meditation and realized in this way. (See Appendix VI).

A spiritual scientific book is not like a toothpaste tube from which, in response to gentle pressure, the "content" flows forth ready for use.

4.

Knowledge and Ability: Knowing and Doing

TO ARRIVE AT higher knowledge which is not informational, one must develop a corresponding level of ability. If knowledge and ability are separate, both tend to decay. Knowledge or wisdom, without the capacity by which it first came about, becomes information, dogma, already-thought thoughts; it turns into teaching on an inadequate plane, formalism. Meditation without cognition leads to merely psychological states, to quietism, to self-involvement, and is meaningless for humanity, the earth, and the universe.

In the history of Zen Buddhism, we find repeated historical demonstrations of the struggle for cognitive meditation.[4] The old Zen masters knew of the danger of communication, and wanted to preempt it by non-communication. So-called negative theology, from Dionysius the Areopagite to Nicholas of Cusa, behaved similarly, avoiding saying anything about the divine except negatively—not this, not that; *neti, neti.* But the Zen masters also knew the danger of noncognitive meditation. The danger of communication lies in the possibility of its becoming autonomous, with the result that it replaces experience instead of leading to it—and people are content with the communication alone. On a lower plane, this resembles the attitude of a person satisfied with a description of the letters, without trying to read them together; or of a person looking at a map without experiencing the geographical place. The letters are directives to realize them. And so too are the communications of spiritual investigation: one cannot treat them as information. We are all too used to taking texts as information—which is far easier than transforming them back into the experience from which they stem.

Today, because of the communication of spiritual scientific research, we can have knowledge without ability. At the same time, through meditative practices inappropriate to westernized humanity (meaning all who have grown up in Western civilization), meditative forms that do not lead to cognition are now widespread. We have exactly what all the progressive traditions wanted to avoid: *Prajna* (wisdom) without *Dhyana* (meditating) and *Dhyana* without *Prajna*.

In the era of the intellectual soul, the soul's structure made it impossible to speak about something without being able to think it completely. This is quite possible, however, for the consciousness soul for in it thinking has emancipated itself from language[5]. The fact that the language of the spiritual scientific communication is everyday language contributes to this; mathematics has its own language so that it cannot be misunderstood or misinterpreted.

In a scientific presentation, reliance on a cited text, on an authority, cannot be an argument. Every assertion is to be verified or understood: that makes what has been communicated into science. Wherever we *refer* to a teaching, dogmas, or traditions—if it is not a case of indicating a train of thought for the sake of brevity—we are dealing with something nonreproducible. For we would not need to refer to anything if we ourselves could reproduce its content. In other words, it is not a question of cognizing, but of something that someone else, at some other time, once cognized—which we do not understand or are uncertain of. Otherwise, it would be current, actual cognition—our own. We rely on something, or on someone, when we cannot cognize for ourselves.

Every reference to or reliance on something else is therefore illusory. For in the end we have to decide for ourselves on what or on whom to rely and to whom to refer. This decision is a much more demanding task than the person making the reference can achieve. The decision about what to rely on—who or what to refer to—cannot come from cognition, for then this cognition would also have to be able to judge the source of what is to be relied on. This task is necessarily greater than the cognitive task in place of which we attempt to rely on something else.

Once again, naive realism is at work here. A person who has recourse to an authority does not notice that he or she is doing the choosing—does not notice that it is they who are calling what is being referred to valid or true. Such a person does not stand on the ground of cognizing. On the other hand, if we are based in cognizing, then we have the certainty of finding truth, even if not right away. Otherwise, we quickly fall into traditionalism, fanaticism, dogmatism, dependence on authority—all of which are forms of naive realism.

5.

Enslavement

WHENEVER IT INVOLVES itself in the communications of the spiritual researcher, naive intellectualism is usually led by an unconscious feeling that guarantees the truth of the contents. Intellectualism easily goes astray with these contents, however, which it is not competent to understand. And in this way the feeling that initially guided it is also corrupted, because inadequate understanding hinders its streaming into the contents. Therefore the contents soon become cold, abstract, dead – as befits the intellect. Cognitive feeling, because it is lacking, is often replaced by sentimentality, the opposite of feeling, which enters through a kind of sentimental effusion, enthusiasm, or *schwärmerei*. (See Appendix VII) This *schwärmerei* invariably seeks the "spirit" in those areas where nonunderstanding reigns and science still has to make something clear.

Inadequate intellectual cognition prevents cognitive feeling from developing. Rejected, cognitive feeling then decays into the egotistical gesture of pride in "knowing" the supposed esoteric contents, which appear esoteric only to sentimental enthusiasm or *schwärmerei*. In truth, there are no esoteric *contents* (= information), there are only esoteric *capacities*. The incorporation of such contents, when they have not been made transparent in the right way, leads to further injuries to consciousness.

One of the most important of these is enslavement by "ideas" that are accepted as truths without being experienced, i.e., without their being understood or realized. And ideas of a higher kind can only be experienced by a consciousness whose capacities have been heightened. "One must be able to face the idea *in experience*, otherwise one falls under its domination."[6] "Every idea that does not become your ideal kills a force in your soul; but every idea that becomes your ideal creates life-forces within you."[7] With regard to a cognitive idea, the "ideal" can only consist in producing the idea oneself, i.e., reproducing it in one's understanding.

By means of the study of spiritual scientific communications, one seeks to overcome one's own narrowed understanding and attain new, better, and higher cognitive capacities above and beyond it. But how can that happen if, during the process, one uses *only* the same understanding as before?

In studying or reading, a point must be reached when schooling of consciousness can begin. Study, however, must not be thought of as an activity of the memory. To come to "know" what is in a spiritual scientific communication is empty illusion, since it contains no information. If high-level communications are "summed up," i.e., formulated and repeated by the intellect, then they are reduced to a level where they become "distorted truths." Then they do no service to the subject, the summarizer, or the listeners. It occurs to no one (we hope) to "summarize" the prologue to the Gospel of St. John. We sin irreverently against the holiness of the texts by handling them with the everyday intellect.

Another example of this behavior is the attempt to explain symbols. If symbols were explicable, they would not be symbols, or else they would be superfluous. The same applies to the "interpretation" of fairy tales and myths. Just as a poem cannot be rendered in other words, and just as music cannot be put into words, so too fairy tales, myths, and the communications of spiritual research cannot be reproduced.

Steiner characterizes the first stage of the modern cognitive path as "study." From the above, one can see that this is not to be understood as the gathering of knowledge. I shall try to show in chapter 7 how study, in Steiner's sense, could be shaped.

Spiritual science cannot in truth be approached without a change in the everyday self. Without such a change, spiritual science is not possible as a science – a science that calls for, and applies, higher cognitive capacities. It is the goal of spiritual science to change us, and it offers methods to do so.

If spiritual science is worked with in any other way, then one is denying in practice what one recognizes theoretically, namely that there are other, higher levels of consciousness beyond the everyday level. (See Appendix VII)

6.

Temptation

MEETING SPIRITUAL SCIENCE exposes a person to two temptations. Both result from taking the teaching not as science of the spirit but as something lying in between religion and science. The "feeling for truth" shifts them in the direction of religion while the "contents" shifts them in the direction of science or knowledge. The right approach would be adequate cognition leading to cognitive religion. Steiner characterizes it thus:

"We must retrieve and experience in full consciousness the soul-orientation of primordial humanity. Then we would achieve a religious cognition, a cognitive religion, for modern human beings." [8]

The first temptation—the shift toward religion—can be seen as something human-all-too-human. The other primary temptation—the shift toward knowledge—must be recognized as something specific to the occult. It leads to the teaching becoming, through human beings, open to adversarial powers that take command of it and twist it into its opposite. Instead of completing the work and developing it further, a hypocritical adherence to the text and authority of the one—and only—spiritual researcher develops out of revolutionary, inner activity directed toward freedom. Distortion already occurs when the communications are lowered to the everyday or scientific level of consciousness. This becomes possible when the texts become independent, when they are separated as texts from the experience of them. A person caught in this process fails to notice what he or she is doing: this demonstrates the temptation-quality, since theoretically anyone could know that it is a matter of contents that transcend everyday consciousness. To speak about what one has never experienced, as if one could understand it and produce it oneself, is impossible in any other field. The power and felt truth of the encountered world-picture misleads us into trying to proselytize before we have fully and really penetrated it. Speaking about what we have not adequately understood hardens the enclosures that arise in consciousness because of inappropriate receptivity. (See Appendix IX)

This occult temptation was avoided in more silent times and places by the refusal to communicate. This was the case in Zen and in negative theology. But the time we live in brings new spiritual capacities with each generation, and these new capacities demand a teaching regarding the region into which they extend. If this is not given, the capacities can easily become spoiled and spoil the human being. Communication is therefore necessary, and the risk of misunderstanding and of the degeneration of the teaching must be accepted. Work with the teaching is entrusted to human freedom.

The obstacle posed by the use of normal language for the communication of spiritual research can be overcome by using words in a particular way. Words may be placed in a meditative text in such a way that the text can be understood on many levels. However, the reader or listener must not be satisfied with understanding on the level of everyday consciousness. The occult temptation of speaking about what one has not experienced continually blends into the first temptation: the egotistical use of spiritual science. This happens when people seek recognition, position, power, or their living through spiritual science or knowledge of spiritual science. They forget the way of life of the old Rosicrucians who, besides cultivating their spiritual origins, had a profession in life.

When a person is unaware of abusing spiritual science for egotistical ends, this has consequences: there is a disorientation with regard to the relationship between spiritual science and everyday life; a loss of the capacity to distinguish, in judgment, between what one understands and does not understand; and the acquiring of the tendency to bluff with contents one has read, using these as arguments and quoting them dialectically in discussions. Because these contents are used on this everyday level, they become interspersed, even confused, with impulses and associations from the subconscious. "Work" with "contents" degenerates into speculation, combination, rhetoric, and nominalistic usage. One begins to receive the contents in "sleepy ecstasy,"[9] and thereby increasingly loses one's healthy feeling for the truth—which is then replaced by pride, superiority, and the air of knowing better than anyone else. Simultaneously, no new spiritual research arises, and therefore no new results. One begins to "live" out of the communications of the founder of spiritual science. This is a kind of spiritual parasitism which creates nothing new and *returns nothing* of what has been received. Anyone seeking to bring something new is then looked at askance: he or she is suspected of falsifying the teaching. Outwardly, such a person becomes untrustworthy—for it is not long before attentive listeners realize their own lack of experience. Admittedly, it can often happen that personalities who, through predisposition or through experiences (for example, through drugs), tend toward a loosening from the body, enliven spiritual-scientific "contents" with a noncognizing, half-free feeling and, by a kind of resonance, find a following, especially among those who have "practiced" spiritual science abstractly and with inadequate concepts. In the right circumstances, one can fool oneself and others in this way for a time. Among the secret goings-on that then occur, "esoteric" groups are formed, generally with the inclusion of ceremonial, ritual activities which speak powerfully to subconscious tendencies.

The problem of how to do spiritual research *without* spiritual capacities occupies many adherents of spiritual science. Attempts to "solve" this are numerous. The real solution, however, would be precisely to develop spiritual capacities. For, with the powers that have been given or left us, we can immediately neither achieve nor communicate real, effective wisdom – wisdom that is worth the effort. Otherwise we would all be sages and initiates, and everything would have been communicated in the course of the ages. Yet human beings were and still are too weak to understand what has been communicated. We all experience the results of this. Whitewashing the situation only darkens the prospect still further.

7.

Right Study

IF STUDY, in the context of spiritual science, meant what it usually does, namely the acquisition of knowledge in the normal way, then it would be a hindrance to the development of higher cognitive capacities, as indeed it often is. Normal consciousness would enrich itself with new, "occult" contents and hang on to itself all the more. Actually, however, the right study and reading of spiritual-scientific communications serves as a preparation for acquiring spiritual capacities. The reader notices the insufficiency of his everyday (and scientific) concepts and attempts to grasp new, higher concepts through thought-intuitions. This is precisely the first goal: to loosen and replace one's normal conceptual system (to which one clings and through which one maintains one's habitual world) with new ideas. The concepts we need are characterized as living, fluid, unfinished. (See Appendix X)

Attentive readers will soon notice that spiritual scientific texts are largely inaccessible without consciousness-exercises, because "healthy human understanding" is not available to them (See Appendix IX). They will also notice that the imagistic language used to portray spiritual experiences ought not to lead to *ideas* (mental representations, *Vorstellungen*), but rather offers the stuff of *meditation*. Meditative practice and meditative reading as the form of study are introduced through the formation of higher concepts, and these lead gradually to the exercise and pursuit of pure thinking.

That is the goal of study according to Steiner. (See Appendix XII) As Steiner puts it:

> Studying is not learning as this usually occurs. Rather we must come to recognize that a thinking that is still fluid, real thinking is available to us, thinking in which we exclude all surrounding sense-perceptions.... Without becoming an empty vessel, we must learn to forget everything, to disregard everything that has an effect on the senses from outside. This is possible if we immerse ourselves in a pure thought free of sensuality (we may find such a thought in the communications of the spiritual researcher) and if we ponder what is unfolded there .... Whoever wants to move higher must read spiritual scientific communications in this way. Whoever does not want to move higher can read them like a normal book.[10]

In the latter case, when we read a spiritual-scientific communication as we read a normal book, there is no question of "study" in the sense of the first step on the cognitive path. The next stage on the cognitive path is the attainment of imagination. This presupposes practice in meditation on the preceding, initial stage of the path.

Higher thinking is also characterized as clairvoyant thinking. (See Appendix XIII) The path to such clairvoyance passes through the experience of thinking, that is of the thinking-process, which normally flows on supraconsciously. (See Appendix XIV) Such thinking is imaginative thinking, which proceeds wordlessly. It makes formulation in a language possible. [11] (See Appendices 15 and 16)

If anthroposophy is a spiritual path, that is, if human beings meet one another at a heightened plane, then the formation of a community, one of the greatest questions in any grouping, becomes not a difficulty but rather something self-evident. (See Appendix XVII)

Spiritual science should be science, not a substitute for religion, not obscurantism, not a collection of the not-understood and the not-understandable. This is what our time demands. "For in our time cognitive value can be ascribed to a way of thinking only if it can justify its views in the face of the same criticism with regard to which natural scientific laws seek their justification."[12] (See Appendices XVIII and XIX)

Afterword

1. The Transmission of Anthroposophy

For about a hundred and fifty years public statements have been made regarding higher cognitive realms. An outline of the forms of communication was given in chapter 1. Because of rapidly changing predispositions in consciousness, new forms of communication must be continually found. (Every teacher knows how fast these predispositions change over time: the method of teaching must be renewed every five to ten years.)

Although Steiner himself could still count on his language of images (*Theosophy, Occult Science, Knowledge of Higher Worlds and Its Attainment*) being understood by a readership schooled in theosophy, the capacity for taking this language at its symbolic value has rapidly declined and today has almost disappeared. This may not be very noticeable in an established anthroposophical environment, but it certainly contributes to the slowness with which spiritual science spreads. Where anthroposophy is introduced in public in its historical beginnings, it is quickly rejected for its pictorial-representational form. Because this form of imagistic language is misunderstood, anthroposophy cannot satisfy the claim to be scientific. This works against the great attractive power of the truth which is what *gives meaning* in spiritual scientific teaching. Cosmology, history, human life, all receive their meaning from the power of the truth and everyone, especially the young, searches for this meaning with burning intensity at least for a time.

Because of the change in the disposition of consciousness the actual way of communicating—in every field—has shifted toward a person's own experiences of consciousness, which is the appropriate gesture of the consciousness-soul. When communicating, one must start from an audience's or reader's possible experiences and build upon these. Points of contact with spiritual, supraconscious regions of the soul may be found in ordinary consciousness, for example, in the "how" of thinking and perceiving, in "understanding," and in the experience of evidence. Starting with such boundary experiences a safe path for building up spiritual science may be found. Such starting points can be found in each of Steiner's epistemological works. Indeed, to offer such starting points is the real goal of these works. Studying them, the possibility then arises of working out for oneself sufficient knowledge of human nature so that one knows the how and why of the schooling of consciousness. One's study should aim toward this point, in order to be able then to continue it adequately.

Communication is not so difficult when it is a matter of information. It becomes problematic, indeed questionable, when one wants to communicate a *how*, not a *what*. And in spiritual science it is always a question of a *how*, for even in its lowest layers the spiritual world is one of becoming and not one of static being. And if the method of communication is important here, the communicator is incomparably more important. For in this realm one can only legitimately communicate what one has experienced oneself or could experience. Only that will sound believable. Everything else may fascinate for a time, but soon the question of authenticity will come up. Just as only a mathematician can speak authentically about mathematics, only those persons can speak of spiritual science who have experience in that area, and only to the extent that they have experience. One cannot represent Rudolf Steiner if one does not have his potential for experience; one can only represent oneself with, and to the extent of, one's own experience. Everything else is temptation or giving in to temptation. One's own naive realism—the view that what one has read is something finished and given—contributes to the temptation and to the spread of the misunderstanding—and often to the rejection—of anthroposophy. Therefore it is advisable to begin one's study with an epistemological introduction, which should not be at all philosophical. The general rule of building on accessible experiences applies here too. What has been reached philosophically, by a lengthy path, can become a general experience: "Reality is something that becomes through cognition."[13]

Reality arises through cognition, anew at each moment and for each individual. For this reason cognition in the age of human maturity and responsibility, that is, the age of the consciousness soul, must be *cultivated.* This cultivation—the practice and pursuit of our given potential capacities—has several meanings. First, there is a soul-hygienic or therapeutic meaning: we will not fall ill because of our unused capacities or powers. Second, a hermeneutic, sense-giving meaning; we give our given world, nature, meaning, just as we do a text we read. By this gift nature can be liberated and the world arise anew out of the interiorized powers of wisdom and of human love for what is not yet, for what can be created through love. There is also a meaning creative of the future: this is that we receive more intuitions, more new ideas—without which human life wastes away.

The question may be asked: How does one read and work with an imagistic presentation of supersensible experiences? Can you give an example?

If the "right" way of working could be described, then the imagistic quality would be superfluous or would have only a playful meaning. Nevertheless, we shall note here one of Steiner's own tips[14] – namely when he explained why, in the Old Testament, the Elohim, in their "prohibition," spoke of *trees*, the Tree of Knowledge and the Tree of Life.

Paradise, from which human beings were driven, consisted of life in the sphere of plants and trees. Humanity did not yet live on the "earth," in the mineral sphere, but in the planet's life sphere. The "Fall," understood as an outer event, as a descent into the mineral sphere (3 Genesis speaks very clearly of this) is what began with the first "eating." Previously, humanity had obtained its nourishment through perceiving, breathing and taking in nourishment as a unified process.

Humanity climbed down from the "trees," and not the apes as evolutionary theory claims.

2. On Speculative Anthroposophy

A DEMANDING TEXT can best offer readers the experience that is fundamental to epistemology. This is the experience that a person who understands a text "co-creates" its momentary reality. For, in reading a text, we combine—"read together"—the letters, words, sentences, etc., giving these a meaning, a significance in us that never appears in the sensory world. Thus, we are co-creators of a reality whose raw materials have been *given* to us—perhaps only as the seed of an idea. What is given, however, can never be the *whole* reality.

With regard to a text, there can certainly be no "in itself." The author has already mysteriously concealed meaning and significance in the sensory, perceptible appearance. He or she wanted to say something.

The form of a text's reality alters with each reading because a demanding text changes the reader through the work he or she performs in understanding it. In the process, the text helps the reader to develop new capacities, and the changed reader then sees a different meaning in the text than before. For this to happen, a text must have depth or height, that is, ambiguity (polysemy, multiple meanings) in the vertical sense. In other words, we can immerse ourselves ever more deeply in it and find ever new waves of meaning. That is why demanding texts are ambiguous and lack a consistent terminology; one and the same word can have different meanings throughout the text. This is a characteristic of every original text, whether it be the Bible or the Buddha's sermons or a text by Steiner.

This vertical ambiguity develops because in meditative texts most if not all words are used in their *original meaning*. This original meaning cannot be explained or defined. It makes it possible for a word to be used in very different contexts: for example, the preposition "in" can be used in relation to space or time or in a metaphorical sense ("in love").

Such texts usually move not only the intellect; superconsciously, cognitive feeling also resonates with them.[15] There are fateful encounters with texts. Considering the general disease of modern consciousness, anthroposophical texts would seem to be relevant for everybody in western culture.

Anthroposophy can be taken up in many different ways. This is facilitated by degrees of affinity and demanded by the immediate sense for the truth. It can be understood with a pure heart because it satisfies a heart's need. The understanding that is like a feeling provides a certainty that lasts as long as the magic of the polyphony of the words persists. And this lasts until the reader begins to think or speak about the contents. Then two great questions arise: How are we to process what we have read? and how can we speak about it with others?

At first, our thinking is unprepared for such contents; they derive from spiritual experience and are brought into language through a very complicated process of "translation."[16] For this reason reading requires a "translating back," which is almost never complete. What we are dealing with here are living and cognitively tangible texts that address the reversed will[17]—we are not dealing with information.[18] Our ordinary intellect as well as scientific thinking, however, work on the dialectical plane of unambiguous information. This is the ideal to which scientific texts aspire. For meditative texts such deductive, speculative, comparative, philological thinking is completely out of place.[19]

Thinking and the ability to think are seductive. After all, we can think *everything*, even sentences such as "In the beginning was the Word," which we can even translate into other languages. Nevertheless, it is clear that we think, understand, and translate only the informational content—which can be the *starting point* for higher thinking and understanding. We often hear talk and discussion about hierarchical beings—do we really think them? We cannot think even one ready-made object in nature adequately—not a blade of grass, a pebble, or a flea—and yet we often brazenly utter the names of the angelic orders (Archangel, Dynameis, or Cherubim). Could we distinguish among these beings if they entered the room (disregarding for the moment the fact that we would drop dead if they did)? Thinking is an activity of many levels. To be able to take its power with us to the higher levels, we would have to learn to do it properly on the lowest level and to understand its scope. Meditating has been characterized as the "behavior of a soul powerful in thoughts,"[20] that is, *only* the power of thinking can be used in that soul. All this prompted Steiner to say ". . . some things are hard to bear—but what is hardest to bear for the person who knows the whole human side of supersensible knowledge is when certain people press supersensible knowledge into purely theoretical formulas."[21]

The treasure that has been found—found usually on the basis of feeling—should be assimilated through the metamorphosis of thinking into the experience of thinking.[22] At the same time, to remain in the eternal present with the ideas of the text, the treasure should be purified: purified of emotions, even of positive preconceptions, of sensory elements, and of elements from the past (of thought content). This is what meditative assimilation is. And this is also the minimum requirement for being able to speak of the contents of the text.

The seductive power of speaking prematurely is great and

manifold.[23] One of the reasons is that one would like to pass on the power that gives meaning to all human life. Here the danger of distortion rears its head, for a meditative text cannot be summarized (as the prologue to the Gospel of St. John cannot be condensed). Without experience, the contents of a meditative text remain merely cold words. Warming these contents with subjective feelings further diminishes the quality of the communication. We can present convincingly only what we have experienced ourselves, what we have witnessed, and whose every word we can stand behind. That is why there is the warning—so unpopular with many and so hard to accept—that "those who have learned about these things (the results of spiritual research) only as students from a teacher had better not pass them on under any circumstances! Today it is advisable to pass on only those things one has found out and researched for oneself. To do thus can and must serve all of humanity."[24]

That aside, this speaking about what one has not experienced oneself is an obstacle on the path to experience for the speaker, because the dialectical consciousness, which we are striving to overcome, is strengthened by the contents we have only read about. Besides, this manner of presentation is never convincing.[25]

This may well be the main reason why there are so few anthroposophists. The frequent dilettantism in the sphere of so-called anthroposophical art also does its share. For anthroposophy should now be relevant for hundreds of millions of people—Steiner was of the opinion in the 1920s that two million people were *then* looking for anthroposophy.

Applying the strict standard outlined above, we might get the feeling that one cannot speak about anthroposophy at all. That is wrong, of course. Even Rudolf Steiner himself built up anthroposophy gradually, by stages, in the course of his life, basing it above all on experiences of consciousness that everyone can achieve in the age of the consciousness soul with only a bit of good will. It is the threshold experiences of consciousness that lead us further.[26] Thus, *The Philosophy of Freedom* points to the crossing of the threshold from the observation of past thinking to the experience of present thinking.[27] We can read about threshold experiences in the "Perspectives" in *The Riddles of Philosophy* and in *The Riddle of Man* as well as in the 1918 afterword to *Knowledge of Higher Worlds and Its Attainment.* The written works, such as *The Threshold of the Spiritual World* and *A Path to Self-Knowledge*, introduce us to anthroposophy through experiences of consciousness.

Only an unreflecting naiveté—one that avoids the basic gesture of the consciousness soul—does not see that cognition, whether conscious or not, is the gate through which "contents" enter us and those who listen to us. For this reason cognition should be a properly and adequately prepared gate. Taking into consideration the nature of modern education, particularly the university system, it is not at all certain that the theosophical language of images is really the language in which the being of anthroposophy may be *understood.* For this theosophical language presupposes a meditative working with images; at the very least it calls upon our sense for the truth. This, however, works nowadays very differently from the way it did in Steiner's theosophical time (we must not forget that all the basic works are from that time; that is, they were written for theosophists!) or in the fifties or seventies. Today, this theosophical path of images is blocked more than ever before and, especially when speakers or writers represent it without any experience of their own, that is, when they cannot fully stand behind it, this path is likely to put off those who are called.[28]

The resolution of all the questions discussed here is very simple, yet tremendously difficult. For it requires us to have experiences of our own, to engage in spiritual research, to have active knowledge[29] instead of reasoning and our own research results in the place of compiled passages from Steiner's texts. And aren't conditions today a little like those among the theosophists Steiner once complained about? You will find (he said) that "in these [English-speaking] occult societies people always emphasize the old. The more they can stress that some rite or some dogma is old, the more – please forgive me for using this trivial expression – they lick their fingers and relish it. And when these people want to interest others in their occult science, they announce it as Rosicrucian at the very least or even as Egyptian. In any case, it has to be old. And this corresponds to the fact that those societies do not cultivate any currently and directly acquired knowledge. True, they may be investigating this or that thing directly, albeit according to the rules of an old, antiquated spiritual science. But they actively turn against what is being fostered here: science acquired directly out of the impulses of the present time. That is what those societies oppose with all their might. . . ."[30]

These comments are not intended to exonerate the "approximately thirty different occultist movements" in the immediate vicinity of the Anthroposophical Society.[31] Those who can judge whether a text is true, regardless of who wrote it, will find their way in this jungle. However, those who rely on their naive trust in authority are easily taken in. Particularly people who have become tired of speculative anthroposophy will run after such movements. They will think that they have found the compensating counterbalance in ceremonies, rituals, etc.

Such people seem to have forgotten that on the ascent from the low point of life there can now be only one basic ritual: the sober schooling of a thinking, perceiving, feeling, and willing attention.

For this, all outer gestures are only distractions.

Appendices

I. Understanding Imagistic Descriptions
(cf. chapter 1)

The Threshold of the Spiritual World (GA17), Afterword: "One can certainly describe what one sees in the supersensible world with images drawn from the sensory world. One can, for example, say that a being reveals itself as if in the appearance of a color. Whoever encounters such descriptions of supersensible beings, however, should be careful never to forget that when true spiritual researchers refer to such a color, they mean that they are living through something the psychological experience of which is *like* the sensory perception of this color. Persons who mean by their description that they have something before their consciousness that is the *same* as a sensory color, are not spiritual researchers, but rather visionaries or hallucinators....

"There are people who are disappointed precisely because the spiritual researcher has to tell them that, when he expresses himself through images borrowed from sensory experience, he is only illustrating what he has seen. Such people are not actually striving to know a supersensible world different from the sensory one. What they want, instead, is to acknowledge a kind of double of the sensory world *as* the supersensible one. This supersensible world is supposed to be finer, more "etheric" than the sensory world.

Besides that, it is not supposed to demand of us to be comprehended through different images than the sensory world. Whoever really wants to approach the spiritual world, however, must also take the trouble to acquire new images. Whoever wants to imagine only a thinned-out, vaporous copy of the sensory world cannot grasp the supersensible."

See also *Theosophy* (GA9), Chapter VI, "The Three Worlds."

II. Deductive Reason and the Supersensible
(cf. chapter 1)

Observation of Nature, Mathematics, Scientific Experiment: Cognitive Results from the Point of View of Anthroposophy [The Mathematics Course] (GA324), lecture of March 19, 1921:
"Spiritual science, as we mean it here, does not set great store on such arguments by analogy; it relies only on unmediated seeing. Therefore it must always be emphasized that before speaking about something like the earth as an organism, we must speak about imaginative thinking [Vorstellen], since it is only in imaginative thinking, and not in the deductive, combining intellect with its analogies, that the earth can be given as a whole being."

The Effect of Occult Development upon the Sheaths of Man (GA145), lecture of March 24, 1913:
"One finds more and more that precisely this cleverness, this smartness, has not the slightest value for the real business of the higher, spiritual life – although one must bring it along with one as much as possible from one's starting point, the

physical plane, if one wants to enter on the path to higher worlds."

III. Remembering Contents and the "State of the Soul"

Earthly Knowledge and Heavenly Wisdom (GA221), lecture of February 18, 1923:
"It makes no difference if one says, with the natural scientists, 'Marsupial, man-ape, ape-man, human being' or if one says, 'A human being consists of physical body, etheric body, astral body, and I.' It is only a different thought; the state of the soul is no different. The state of the soul only becomes different if this spiritual understanding of human beings in nature becomes inwardly alive. But this cannot happen unless the same feeling, the same sensation—the same soul state that lives in love—accompanies the cognition."

(Second Religious Course, lecture of September 23, 1921, 2nd discussion hour:
"It is not as if one achieves anthroposophical knowledge and then has it in memory. That changes it into ordinary knowledge. If one has the right relationship to it, then one always has to actually return to it again.")

Die soziale Grundforderung unserer Zeit. In geänderter Zeitlage (*The Social Challenge of Our Times*) (GA 186), lecture of December 12, 1918:
"You will certainly notice that one can do nothing in real spiritual science by memory, by effortless remembering. One forgets things, and has to cultivate them again and again. But just this is good—just this is the right thing—that over and over again one must strive anew. And someone

who is truly advanced in the area of spiritual science will try to review the most elementary things every day; others are ashamed to do this. In spiritual science nothing should depend on noting something in memory, since everything depends upon one's seizing it in the immediate experience of the present."

Ibid. *The Challenge of the Times*, (GA186), lecture of November 29, 1918:
"These methodological things are the most important of all in the area of spiritual scientific cognition, which is so necessary in our time. What this spiritual science makes of our soul is much more necessary than the abstract familiarization with one or another truth."

IV. Healthy Human Understanding

Lebendiges Naturerkennen, intellektueller Sündenfall und spirituelle Sündenerhebung (Living Cognition of Nature, Intellectual Fall and Spiritual Redemption) (GA220), lecture of January 26, 1923:
"To a certain extent, the common consciousness of the present, through a consciousness of the Fall, has itself fallen. Intellectualism today is already characterized by decay. In fact it is characterized by such powerful decay that if the intellectualist culture persists in its current contours, we really cannot speak of humanity reaching its earthly goal. It is necessary to realize today that, in the depths of the human, soul forces still hold sway that are, to a certain extent, better than the consciousness-culture that has taken root so far."

"An essential characteristic of medieval thinking has entered into today's thinking in that we actually only consider thinking as it applies to external nature. We do not really consider process of thought, we do not immerse ourselves in the contemplation of thinking. No one really takes any notice of thinking itself in its inner aliveness."

[The gesture of the consciousness soul, whereby the *processes* of consciousness, not only their results, are held in view, is lacking—G.K.]

"But it is impossible for the evolutionary stream that ended in Darwin and that is still prevalent today in official science to arrive at the truth. For the misunderstood Fall has ruined thinking; it has brought thinking into decay. The situation is really graver than we are inclined to admit."

The Presence of the Dead (GA154), lecture of March 12, 1914:
"Let us try to arrive at an understanding of how the world citizen of today, who is untouched by spiritual science, just as he is, born of the attitudes of the present—how such a person stands in relation to spiritual science. He hears this or that; he hears that people are making this or that claim about spiritual worlds. What must he necessarily do? Well, a human being cannot do otherwise than to try to understand what is said to him with the ideas he already has.... But the ordinary cultured person of our time has no ideas that could make comprehensible to him what is said about the spiritual world by real spiritual science. To begin with, he lacks the appropriate mental pictures, concepts, and ideas. He tries to penetrate what is said with the ideas he has, but these are taken over from altogether other areas. How, then, could he fail to misunderstand these things? How could one expect him to bring any understanding at all to these things?"

Geistige und soziale Wandlungen in der Menschheitsentwickelung (Spiritual and Social Transformations in Human Evolution), (GA196) lecture of January 18, 1920:
"What we lack most in our time is not supersensible experience; what we lack most in our time is healthy logic, that is, really healthy thinking, which is also, above all, the power of truthfulness. The instant that untruthfulness comes to the fore, supersensible experiences melt away, and then human beings can arrive at no understanding of supersensible experiences."

"It is precisely what adapts people to the materialistic age that darkens for them the sphere in which the supersensible worlds approach them. People today are used to thinking in a way that only works in relation to bodily functions. People are trained in this from their youth on. But healthy human understanding does not develop on the basis of the body."

Man in the Light of Occultism, Theosophy and Philosophy (GA137), lecture of June 5, 1912:
"Tireless, orderly thinking is required to see that there exists no truth that contradicts what theosophy is. But such thinking is not only extraordinarily rare, it is also extraordinarily hard to achieve."

Building Stones for an Understanding of the Mystery of Golgotha (GA152), lecture of May 1, 1913:
"...but once they [the truths of spiritual science] have been discovered and expressed in the ordinary, normal language of human reason, they can be understood by every human soul that eliminates the obstacles to such an understanding from itself.... if this soul will only liberate within itself all the moral courage that it possesses, so that it can set aside the obstacles stemming from Ahriman."

Der Mensch als geistiges Wesen im historischen Werdegang (The Human Being as a Spiritual Being in Historical Development (GA206, Part Two), lecture of August 14, 1921:
"Only when experiences of the various worlds are brought into comprehensible ideas of this kind, can one enter into them. But to do so requires that one work one's way up to something that needs no occult schooling: namely, the comprehension of ideas."

"Naturally, most people today cannot do this—and scientists least of all. Scientists are used to ideas only if the ideas are borrowed from the outer world of the senses. At most, they allow themselves mathematics; other than this, they refuse to understand ideas that have to be followed out of themselves. One can follow everything presented by the spiritual scientist if one develops the will to enter into such ideas; one can actually test everything ideationally. But one must will it. This requires precisely ... overcoming what is today assumed to be the recognized, scientific method of thinking, which does not at all coincide with healthy human understanding...."

[The disease of consciousness in the decades following Steiner's death has progressed so far that today one can hardly arrive at "healthy human understanding" without exercises of consciousness of an initially hygienic kind.—G.K.]

Das Geheimnis des Todes (The Secret of Death) (GA159), lecture of June 19, 1915:
"We must be clear that it is not enough if we only intend to be—or simply convince ourselves that we are—beyond all the prejudices of our materialistic age.... These materialistic prejudices cling deeply to our habits of thought, and what clings especially deeply is not materialistic prejudice itself

but what is connected to it. That human beings cannot, in a certain sense, develop a comprehensive capacity for thinking is linked to this materialistic prejudice, the materialistic worldview. However much our age depends upon reason and logic, sharp reason and sharp logic are in fact today very seldom the possession of those who seek to be at the pinnacle of scientific or other cultural endeavors. Clarity of thinking as a whole is not at all striven for in our time."

Aspects of Human Evolution (GA176), lecture of June 26, 1917:
"Healthy human understanding must today be earned by effort, for it is not present . . . It must initially be earned again by acquiring, on paths now given by anthroposophy, what humanity possessed atavistically in earlier times, namely, the connection with the spiritual world – which today is not present atavistically."

[Paths or ways of exercising are clearly indicated here. What demands Steiner made of healthy human understanding are apparent from the next text. – G.K.]

Soziales Verständnis aus geisteswissenschaftlicher Erkenntnis (Social Understanding through Spiritual Scientific Cognition) (GA191), lecture of October 18, 1919:
"As long as you believe that what is out there (i.e., what one sees) is something external, and that what is in here (i.e., in the skull) is something internal, then you cannot possibly arrive at what I always call insight into spiritual scientific facts through healthy human understanding. For you can have insight into spiritual scientific facts only on the basis of unprejudiced observation."

Der innere Aspekt des sozialen Rätsels (The Inner Aspect of the Social Question) (GA193), lecture of June 12, 1919:
"But what does it mean, they [people] don't understand it [spiritual scientific communications]? It means nothing but this: I want to understand spiritual science using only my physical brain; I don't want to learn any other kind of thinking than the one that lazily follows the physical brain. Naturally, the anthroposophical worldview cannot be understood by this kind of thinking. It is not as if one had to be clairvoyant to understand it, but one has to exercise oneself in a kind of thinking that is not bound to the physical brain. And what is present in anthroposophical literature, what can be learned with healthy human understanding—which is not bound to the brain, only unhealthy materialistic understanding is bound to the brain—what can be learned with healthy human understanding gradually trains such thinking, feeling, and willing. And thereby thinking, feeling, and willing become able to cope with the events of the present time."

Philosophy, Cosmology, and Religion (GA215), lecture of September 7, 1922:
"Abstract thinking, which is all people know today, is developed through the instrument of the physical body. It is experienced with the instrument of the physical body. This is the characteristic feature of what humanity has achieved in recent times when it has reached up to full consciousness. A thinking achieved with the physical body is, from the point of view of the spiritual world, actually a displaced thinking.... Because of it, thinking lives in an element that is not its primal element."

Building Stones for an Understanding of the Mystery of Golgotha (GA152), lecture of May 18, 1913:
"Thinking is in every soul, but it can be used in two ways. A human being can create it within himself—can form thoughts within himself. Then this thinking is within his own activity and can fully encounter everything, even the most apparently bold claims of spiritual research. If, however, thinking does not strengthen itself, then it has to depend on the instrument of thinking, the brain, and then it produces only thoughts that can be grasped with the instrument of the brain; then the human being thinks passively, not actively."

Spiritual Science as a Foundation for Social Forms (GA199), lecture of August 7, 1920:
"People, who today want to hold onto the sense world alone, find these anthroposophical thoughts crazy, unreal, fantastic. This is because, at the moment of thinking these thoughts, they have to apply a powerful force: they have to tear themselves free. They want to think these thoughts with their brain. But with the brain one can think only external, physical thoughts; one can think only external physicality. With such thoughts one can certainly think atoms and molecules...; but what is contained in a book like *Occult Science: an Outline* cannot be thought with the brain."

[Healthy human understanding means body-free understanding—G.K.]

Polarities in the Evolution of Mankind (GA197), lecture of September 21, 1920:
"People say that these thoughts cannot be grasped, that they cannot be understood. Well, they want to think them with the brain; but these spiritual scientific thoughts have been

thought by the soul-spiritual element, after it has torn itself free of the brain. Therefore we must strive by means of thoughts that have developed in this way—by thinking these thoughts for ourselves—to tear free our soul-spiritual element from the brain. People must make an effort to think these thoughts through, to avail themselves of the possibility, which still exists today, of tearing free from the matter of the brain what is soul-spiritual. For the soul-spiritual element is beginning to bind itself to the matter of the brain.... When the thoughts of anthroposophically-oriented spiritual science are transmitted to the world, we count on those people who are still capable of managing the old capacity for tearing themselves free; we count on them to actually manage this and to try to understand body-free thoughts so that their souls may become body-free."

V. Pure Thinking

Philosophie und Anthroposophie. Gesammelte Aufsatze 1904-1923 (Philosophy and Anthroposophy. Collected Papers 1904-1923) (GA35), the title essay:
"Suppose you want to form the concept of the circle. One can do this, for example, by going out to the sea to the point where one sees only water in all directions. Then one has formed the image of a circle through perception. But there is another way to arrive at the concept of the circle, and that is by saying to oneself, without any appeal to the senses: I construct for myself mentally all the places that are equidistant from a given point. In order to form this construction, which takes place entirely within the life of thought, one need appeal to nothing external. This is entirely pure thinking in Aristotle's sense, pure actuality."

Philosophy, Cosmology, and Religion (GA215), lecture of September 7, 1922:
"But if, as we experience the merely apparent life of abstract thinking between birth and death – which is pure thinking, nothing but thinking, but thinking as it is carried out by the physical organism – we take moral impulses into this thinking, then these moral impulses live in this pure thinking that has only apparent life and cannot compel us to anything any more than a mirrored image can compel us to some action."

VI. Màntras: Their Origin and Practice

Boundaries of Natural Science (GA322), lecture of October 2, 1920 (evening):
"The mantric art, this living in aphorisms, does not consist in understanding the content of the words behind the aphorism, but rather in experiencing these sayings themselves as something musical. It consists in joining the mantras to one's own soul-power, in staying with the mantra, in strengthening the power of one's own soul by continually saying these phrases over and over to oneself. This mantric art gradually developed to a high degree and transformed the power we normally bear within the soul that enables us to understand another person through the word. It changed this power into a different one. A power lit up in the utterance and repetition of the mantric aphorism, a power that did not now lead over to the other human being, but led within, into the spiritual world. And if one develops the soul through mantras in this way – if one has come so far that inwardly one can feel the weaving and streaming of this soul power, which otherwise remains unconscious because all the attention is directed to understanding the other person through the word – if one has

come so far that one feels this power as a soul-power, as one feels the muscle tension when moving the hand to do something, then one has prepared oneself for grasping what lies in this power, the higher power of thinking."

Geistige Zusammenhänge in der Gestaltung des menschlichen Organismus (Spiritual Relations in the Formation of the Human Organism (GA218), lecture of November 18, 1922:
"As westerners, we no longer strive to experience what is musical in the mantra. We do not vigorously pursue the path the spiritual-psychic element follows as it leaves the body. Rather we follow the subsequent path which takes place when the spiritual-psychic element consciously rejoins the physical organization by taking hold of the physical body.... We achieve this path when—in the same way as we have to take in the I in inspiration—we leave the I outside, while we immerse ourselves again in our corporeality. However, in doing this we do not leave the I unoccupied, or forgotten, or abandoned, or repressed into unconsciousness, but rather we unite just this I with pure thinking, with clear, sharp thinking, so that at least we have the inner experience that our I is thoroughly permeated by all the sharp thinking we have finally achieved."

[When we, as modern human beings, concentrate on something we do not understand in our thinking, then thinking is switched off, put to sleep. Associations, emotions, images from the unconscious arise; and then perhaps other experiences. But none of these are cognitive experiences, nor experiences of a kind that lead to cognitive states of soul—because thinking has remained unexercised, and does not correspond to the experiences, and so can neither cope with nor interpret them. When the I outside the body is permeated with "clear, sharp thinking," this indicates body-free, living thinking, in which the higher I can awaken to self-awareness. At the lowest level sentences that are used for meditation must be *understood* (they cannot be in a language unknown to the meditator) in order to lead the understanding to higher levels where it can live with understanding in the sound of the words. The archaic method also requires an initial apprenticeship to remain within the sounds of the words. Today this is not necessary. Reflective consciousness protects our freedom, since no text or sound can work on us without our permission or contribution. – G.K.]

Karmic Relationships, Volume III, (GA237), lecture of July 1, 1924:
"For following that interval of the darkening of the living element in thinking which then occurred, living thinking must be achieved again, otherwise humanity will remain weak and lose its own reality in relation to the reality of thinking. Therefore it is necessary that following the entry of our Christmas impulse into the anthroposophical movement there should be unreserved speaking in the form of living thinking. Otherwise we shall all the time approach the situation – which we already know here and there – in which the knowledge, for instance, that the human being has a physical, etheric, and an astral body will only be known in the form of dead thinking. But it must not be understood with dead thinking; for, if it is, then it is actually a distorted truth, not the truth itself."

VII. Enthusiasm and Mysticism

Individuelle Geistwesen und ihr Wirken in der Seele des Menschen (Individual Spirit Beings and Their Working in the Human Soul) (GA178), lecture of November 11, 1917:
"The present way of looking at things, which is still infected with materialism even in these areas, loves nothing better than to swim around mystically, unclearly, in all kinds of concepts that have not been thought through."

Die spirituellen Hintergründe der äusseren Welt. Der Sturz der Geister der Finsternis (The Spiritual Underpinnings of the External World. The Fall of the Spirits of Darkness) (GA177), lecture of October 1, 1917:
"One can certainly experience that precisely in spiritual scientific lectures—and sometimes also in pseudo-spiritual scientific lectures—people want to listen in a sleepy ecstasy. They are not really interested in the content particularly, but rather they listen 'warmed by devotion' for the voluptuous pleasure effected by the emergence of the etheric and astral bodies. In other life circumstances this being 'warmed by devotion' can be very good—but for disclosing certain spiritual things, it is completely useless!"

[The development of higher cognitive capacities requires a mathematical precision—G.K.]

Fruits of Anthroposophy (GA78), lecture of September 3, 1920:
"All [the rules given by Steiner] have the aim that whatever is done by a person who strives to develop a higher cognitive ability is done with the same inner clarity required for the

development of mathematical ideas. Consciousness must be in the same state as when doing geometry when it lives itself into all that is necessary to build up imagination and the further stages of supersensible cognition, inspiration and intuition. . . .The path to imagination should not be attempted with a lowered consciousness; for one cannot attain to higher cognitions by attempting in a dreamy, mystical, confused, or darkened way what must be attempted in a purely soul-spiritual way with mathematical clarity. . . ."

Was wollte das Goetheanum und was soll die Anthroposophie? (What Was the Goetheanum For and What Should Anthroposophy Be?) (GA84), lecture of April 9, 1923:
"Everything that I describe must be carried out, during the soul-exercises I refer to, in the same way that a mathematician works out his problems. So the person carries out everything in full awareness. Nothing is present in the way of any false mysticism, dreaminess, suggestion, or anything like that. One must set up one's exercises within the soul with the same, let's say, cold sobriety—for the warmth and enthusiasm come about through what one then sees, not through the method—with the same cold sobriety, I say, with which one solves geometric problems."

VIII. "Explanation" of "Contents"

Steiner rejected any attachment to the images and "contents" given by him. He really meant these to be taken in the same way as the founding gesture of the Waldorf pedagogy. He meant to offer something unfinished, that had to be completed by the recipient, as a roughly finished doll kindles the imagination of a child. He often experienced the opposite with people who were working with anthroposophy. In these cases he was tolerant, without accepting the procedure. Thus he said on April 4, 1923 (*Earthly Knowledge and Heavenly Wisdom* GA221):

"Sometimes people get strange ideas from reading anthroposophical books. I can understand these ideas, and usually do not refute them because they are of a certain value for the person having them. For example, concerning my book *An Outline of Occult Science*, some people have had the idea of illustrating it so that it could be presented in pictures, and they thought that they would be doing the book a favor with this. This yearning arose. In fact, people have often shown me samples of such pictures. I have nothing against that; if the sample pictures are good, we can admire them, and it is certainly nice to paint such pictures. But what is the longing that gave rise to this idea? It is the longing to take away the most important thing that can be developed through reading *An Outline of Occult Science*, and instead to present people with pictures that once again board up the world for them.

"What matters most in reading this book is not to rebel against what civilization has brought us—in spite of the decline of our language and the awful state of writing and publishing nowadays, but to accept it in such a way that, in reading, we overcome all this and go beyond it to creating on our own the pictures that are presented in the awful printer's ink in the book. The more unique and individual the pictures each reader is able to create in his or her mind, the better. However, if somebody else draws these pictures for the readers, he boards up the world for them, so to speak. Of course, I do not want to deliver a lecture against painting what is presented in imaginations in *An Outline of Occult Science*, but I do want to point out that everybody needs to have the experience of having to take it in actively."

Before this, Steiner had said:

"When you read the first chapter of *Riddles of the Soul*, regardless of how imperfectly it may be written, you will see my intention in writing it. I wanted to help people realize that if they remain stuck at the level of our present civilization, the world will be boarded up for them. We can only progress so far with the natural sciences, then we come to where the world is as though boarded up. That first chapter was my attempt to clear away the boards. If you feel that you are pulling away the boards that have been enclosing the world for centuries now – when you can regard the words in my book as tools for this pulling away – then you are really approaching the soul-spiritual element. Most people only have an unconscious feeling that chapters such as this are written with pen and ink. Indeed, they are not written with a pen, but with soul tools intended to tear away those boards, that is, to clear away the limits of natural science, but to clear them away through inner soul work. When you read such a chapter, you too must be active and work in your soul."

IX. Temptation

Polarities in the Evolution of Mankind (GA197), lecture of June 24, 1920:

"What anthroposophy has led to [the various applications, Waldorf schools, threefold social order, etc.] will succeed. But if certain things do not change, then what anthroposophy has led to will devour the original spiritual movement. Then we shall have – by the will of the so-called bearers of this spiritual movement—a new materialism, since the spiritual movement at its base is aborted. The spirit must be tended, or else it dies. Materialism does not exist by itself, alone and of its own accord; you cannot create materialism, anymore than you can create a corpse. A corpse arises when the soul leaves the organism. In the same way everything created here from spiritual foundations, from what is ensouled, will become something purely material if the inclination to really nurture the spiritual is absent."

Ibid., lecture of July 25, 1920:
"You see, it is not enough today to rectify—to correct—the so-called worldviews that are floating around. If one wants to be a spiritual scientist, it is actually a matter of completing a real process in oneself, and of not being content with something intellectual or rational or theoretical."

[The reality of the spirit has nothing to do with content—G.K.]

Ibid. lecture of July 30, 1920:
"It is much more important for the total effect of world evolution that a brilliant materialist exists, who represents materialism brilliantly—for it takes spirit to do so, and sometimes it takes very little spirit to plead for a dull mysticism. The dull mystic can, in certain circumstances, contribute much more to the materialization of the world than the brilliant materialist. It is a question of the qualities of the spiritual. That this is recognized is much more important than its contents. This is what has to be learned; for we do not want to achieve spirit as a logical system, but we want to achieve it in its reality. And so I ask, Could not the spirit live in the spirited materialist more than in the dull spiritualist? These things have to be understood and realized by anthroposophically

oriented spiritual science. It is a question of the reality of the spirit, not of the abstract assertion of this or that. People forget precisely this, how much it really is a question of realities, and not of theories!"

[What is at issue is not theories, but spiritual deeds, the transformation of thinking in its givenness, in its dependence on the brain. – G.K.]

Ibid., again the lecture of July 30, 1920:
"Western people are simply on their way to becoming beings that think only with their physical brains. . . . People have become accustomed to thinking merely with the physical brain; that is the normal way to think today. Everything in our normal literature, in our entire modern science, is material thinking, is this kind of thinking. . . ."

"Therefore it is not a question of replacing an old insight or cognition with a new one, but rather a question of achieving cognition as a deed, an act. This protects the soul from being locked into mere materialism; protects the soul-spiritual element from being locked into the ahrimanic (whereby the I would be suspended). Thus, it is not a question of refuting materialism, but rather of protecting humanity from materialism's becoming right; for materialism is on the way to being right, not wrong. . . . It is a question of making materialism incorrect; because materialism, since it is not merely a false theory, is on its way to becoming a fact. . . . It is not because it is false that we have to overcome this materialism with words that remain theory; we must overcome it because it is correct, we have to combat its existence precisely as something correct. This gives things a different aspect. We do not stand in the reality of the spiritual world with theories but with cognitions that are deeds in relation to the cosmos."

Heilfaktoren für den sozialen Organismus (Curative Factors for the Social Organism (GA198), lecture of July 4, 1920:
"The task today is not to overcome a theoretical view; the task today is to overcome the fact that the human soul has become dependent on the body. The task today is not to refute materialism. It is rather to do the work, the soul-spiritual work, that releases the soul once again from the bonds of the material."

[The danger of a rhetorical, intellectual, or speculative anthroposophy, is here portrayed in drastic terms. – G.K.]

Earthly Knowledge and Heavenly Wisdom (GA221), lecture of February 4, 1923:
"Therefore if today a refutation of something in anthroposophy appears, and then a written defense is made with the same means as the refutation, then nothing has been achieved, really nothing at all has been achieved, since people are talking back and forth with the same kind of thinking. This makes no difference; what makes a difference is that anthroposophy should be carried by a new life."

Awakening to Community (GA257), lecture of February 27, 1923:
"Is it then truth, if we speak about the supersensible world and are not in a position to raise ourselves up to grasp this kind of real spirituality, this kind of reversed cult? We only really stand within the understanding, the grasping, of the spiritual when we not only have the idea of the spiritual abstractly, and can reproduce it theoretically – can even reproduce it theoretically for ourselves – but when we can believe (but believe on the basis of an evidential belief that is its own proof) that spirits have spiritual communion with us in spiritual

understanding. You cannot evoke the anthroposophical forming of community through external arrangements. You have to evoke it out of the deepest sources of human consciousness itself."

Die Mission der neuen Geistesoffenbarung. Das Christus-Ereignis als Mittelpunktsgeschehen der Erdenevolution (The Mission of the New Spiritual Revelation. The Christ-Event as the Central Occurrence of Earth Evolution) (GA127), lecture of June 5, 1911:
"It is better to make a mistake honestly than to depend on dogmas dishonestly."

X. New Concepts

The Presence of the Dead, (GA154), lecture of May 12, 1914:
"We talk, for instance, about beings of the higher hierarchies.... We talk about the souls of those who have died.... But we have to be clear as it were with each step that we cannot speak about these things with concepts to be found in the world today. If we do, nothing can come of it but misunderstandings."

The Threshold of the Spiritual World (GA17), chapter "On Knowing the Spiritual World":
"Insight into the results of spiritual science is facilitated if one focuses on what in the normal life of the soul offers concepts capable of being extended and transmuted so as gradually to reach up to the processes and beings of the spiritual world. If one does not patiently choose this path, then one is easily tempted to imagine the spiritual world as much too similar to the physical or sensory world. Indeed,

without this path, one will not even be able to bring about a fitting representation of the spiritual itself and of its relationship to human beings."

[Processes of consciousness, particularly cognitive processes, are indicated here; as an example, a discussion of memory follows. — G.K.]

Awakening to Community (GA257), lecture of March 3, 1923:
"...one can read such a book as, for example, my *Theosophy* in two different ways. One can read in such a way as to read in it that the human being consists of physical, etheric, and astral bodies, etc.; that he has repeated earth lives, karma — in other words, one acquires concepts. To be sure, these are different concepts than in another field, but the spiritual process can be exactly the same as the one that takes place when one reads a cookbook. For I have often said just this: it is a question of the spiritual process, not of acquiring ideas. It is all the same, whether you read that you should pour butter into a pan, add flour, stir, add eggs — or whether you read that there is physical matter, etheric forces, astral forces, which are all mixed together. It is really all one, as a soul process, whether you have mixed together butter, fat, eggs, flour on a stove, or whether you imagine physical body, etheric body, astral body mixed together for the human being.

But one can also read *Theosophy* in such a way that one knows that there are concepts contained there that are related to the normal conceptual world of the physical in the same way that the conceptual world of the physical is related to the dream world. They belong to a world into which one must awaken out of the normal physical world, just as one awakens into the physical world out of the dream world."

Chance, Providence, and Necessity (GA163), lecture of September 6, 1915:

"Even though we want to approach the spiritual world, we often feel the need, or have the yearning, to find these spiritual worlds very similar to the physical worlds, or at least we want to be able to characterize them in such a way that we come out of them with mental pictures familiar to us from the physical world. But I have already often pointed out that the mental pictures we take from the physical world are inadequate for the characterization of the spiritual worlds."

Meditative Betrachtungen und Anleitungen zur Vertiefung der Heilkunst (Meditative Considerations and Suggestions On Deepening the Art of Healing) (GA316), lecture of January 9, 1924:

"If the human being permeates his normal sensory experiences with thoughts as he has them in normal life and carries these thoughts with him into the spiritual world beyond the threshold, then he calls forth before his spiritual eye an illusion. By judging the things beyond the threshold in the same way one looks at or judges things here, one calls forth a real illusion. And this is why that spiritual being is there at the threshold, from whom we can learn that we need altogether different concepts if we are to cross over the threshold. If we cross over into the spiritual world with our normal concepts, taken from the sense world, then that illusion lames us for life. This guardian of the threshold is really the warner, who lets us know we must first create for ourselves the ideas we need in the spiritual world. Normally, people do not believe that the concepts suited to something in the spiritual world are extremely different from the concepts suitable to something here in the physical world."

[The necessary concepts are characterized as follows – G.K.]

Die Wissenschaft vom Werden des Menschen (The Science of Humanity's Becoming) (GA183), lecture of August 4, 1918:
"...the concepts necessary to grasp again the true reality of human beings, and thereby to some extent to understand the true reality of the world, must be fluid; these concepts must not be sharply contoured. For reality is not something static, but something that becomes. And if we want to grasp reality with our concepts and ideas, then we must follow with our concepts the stream, the becoming, of reality."

Geschichtliche Notwendigkeit und Freiheit (Historical Necessity and Freedom) (GA179), lecture of December 15, 1917:
"People often suffer from conceiving as much as possible of what is contained in the spiritual world in terms of space. Even if they conceive of it as nebulous, thin and mist-like, they would like to think of it as spatial in some way: they would like to imagine souls that fly around in space and things like that. If however we really want to penetrate these things we must go beyond the concepts of space and time to more complex concepts."

Man and the World of Stars (GA219), lecture of December 17, 1922:
"But, on the other hand, in what we call anthroposophical spiritual science, we strive to leave the spatial. To be sure, we can somewhat gratify our longings for the spatial by symbolizing the spiritual in sensory terms. That can happen, of course, as an aid to the faculty of mental representation. But we must always remain aware that this is only a sensory image, and that what really matters is a striving, at

least it would have to be a striving, to come out of the spatial.... We strive into what is temporal and also into the supratemporal, into what leads out of the sensory realm altogether."

Spiritual Science as a Foundation for Social Forms (GA199), lecture of August 20, 1920:
"In order to think the spiritual one must make an effort to overcome space itself in one's thinking. Otherwise we will never arrive at what is really spiritual, and, above all, we will never attain even an approximately correct natural science, to say nothing of a spiritual science."

Aspects of Human Evolution (GA176), lecture of July 24, 1917:
"Spiritual science puts in the place of finished concepts, finished mental pictures, something that the soul must repeatedly work on anew; something that the soul must join with over and over again. If we have a good memory, we can receive the external truths as given to us by natural science, once (and for all) and then possess them—because natural scientific truths are given in concepts that are, to a certain extent, dead. Natural laws, as concepts, are dead. Spiritual scientific concepts must be given in living concepts. If we condemn spiritual scientific truths to dead concepts, if we take them in in the way we take in natural truths, then they are not food for the soul but stones for the soul, which cannot be digested.... This is certainly something about spiritual science that leaves many people unsatisfied, since they would like to have something finished. Spiritual science can only give an introduction to "eating the spiritual," but such people would like to have finished food...

Much of what lives . . . as disease in our souls can only be healed when we become interested in the living process of a "life with truth" without becoming greedy for finished truths. Clearly outlined truths, however – indeed, whatever one expresses in finished concepts – always relate to something *past*. In some way or other, what is stamped in finished concepts is always in relation to something past."

XI. First Steps

Supersensible Man [The Supersensible Human Being, Understood Anthroposophically] (GA231), lecture of November 16, 1923:
"I describe this . . . in order . . . to make you aware that the fruits of the spiritual science intended here do not only depend on one's producing them oneself. If one has produced something in a given area, then one knows about producing it. And everyone can reach this point if he keeps in mind to some little extent what I have described, for example, as soul exercises, meditation, concentration, etc., in my book *Knowledge of the Higher Worlds and its Attainment*. If one undertakes the inner soul activity for even only a few of the steps that lead into life, then one opens one's heart to what can be received from the spiritual researchers called to the task. And then the spiritual gift that is received becomes something that can unite deeply with what is personal, because it speaks to what is personal in the human being. Thereby one comes with what is personal in oneself to the sources of that life from which the eternal, in its essence, derives."

Earthly Knowledge and Heavenly Wisdom (GA221), lecture of February 3, 1923:

"People who want to be anthroposophists—and not simply accept anthroposophical thoughts passively but really assimilate them—must pour what they have been during their dreamless sleep into the pure thoughts of anthroposophy with the help of their strong will. Those people will then have reached the first stage of what we can legitimately call clairvoyance. Then they live clairvoyantly in the thoughts of anthroposophy.

"Anthroposophical books must be read with a strong will and we must bring more than just our waking life to them. We must not read anthroposophical books in the way we usually read....

"To read anthroposophical books, we must really enter into them with our whole being. Since we are unconscious during sleep and have no thoughts then—though our will is, of course, still there—we must put our whole will into the reading of anthroposophical books. If you make the contents of an anthroposophical book the object of your will, then you will become immediately clairvoyant, at least in your thoughts, through the exercise of your will....

"We need to find the way from a merely passive, intellectual experiencing of anthroposophical truths to an immersion in them with our whole being. Then anthroposophical teaching will no longer be presented in a deadbeat and feeble way with phrases like 'anthroposophical sources have assured us....' Instead, people will be able to proclaim anthroposophical truths out of their own experience, at least in the most accessible areas, such as medicine, physiology, biology, and the social sphere.

"While we cannot yet reach the sphere of the higher hierarchies on that first level of clairvoyance, nevertheless we can make the spirit in our immediate surroundings the subject of our state of soul. It is a matter of will in the most comprehensive sense whether or not there will be people in our Anthroposophical Society who can give testimony — and we need a valid, living testimony based on their own direct experience of a living source of truth — of the inner truth of anthroposophy."

XII. Study as a Way to Pure Thinking

Das christliche Mysterium (The Christian Mystery) (GA97), lecture of November 30, 1906:
"Study requires that the student have the patience to attain certain concepts about the world. . . . A certain training of the thinking is required, an acclimatization to living and weaving within the pure element of thinking. Books such as *The Philosophy of Freedom* and *Truth and Science* have been written for those who wish to achieve Rosicrucian initiation and wish to train the spirit. What is involved is the overcoming of the difficulties (infinite for many people) involved in following the thoughts and coming to know how one thought develops necessarily out of the other."

Ibid., lecture of February 16, 1907:
"Study, as it is now introduced to human beings, leads away from the world that appeals to the senses. It consists in schooling one's thoughts — so that these then have nothing to do with what surrounds us in the sensory world."

Supersensible Knowledge (GA55), lecture of March 14, 1907:
"[In study]) however it is a question of a thinking that has become free from everything sensory. . . . This thinking is

called in spiritual science and also in Rosicrucianism, "self-engendering thinking."

At the Gates of Theosophy (GA56), lecture of September 4, 1906:
"In study, it is not so much a matter of *what* as of *how*. Through the great truths, as for example, the planetary laws, we create great lines of thinking for ourselves, and this is the essential part of the matter."

The Theosophy of the Rosicrucian (GA99), lecture of May 6, 1907:
"Study, in the Rosicrucian sense, is the ability to become absorbed in a thought content that is taken not from physical reality but from the higher worlds. This is called living in pure thoughts. . . .

[Many people] would rather acquire beautiful feelings; they do not want to study seriously. But no matter how many beautiful feelings one acquires for one's soul, it is impossible by that means alone to ascend to higher worlds. Rosicrucian theosophy does not seek to arouse feelings but, rather, to let the feelings resonate with the powerful facts of the spiritual worlds. The Rosicrucian feels it as a kind of shamelessness to rush at people with feelings. He guides them into the course of human becoming, taking it for granted that feelings will then arise by themselves. He allows the wandering planets to arise before them in the universe, and if the soul experiences these facts, then it should be powerfully affected in its feelings. It is just an evasion if people say one should turn directly to the feeling. That is just laziness."

Die Erkenntnis der Seele und des Geistes (Cognition of the Soul and of the Spirit (GA56), lecture of November 28, 1907:
"No one should develop feeling before he has brought sensory-free thinking up to a certain level."

XIII. Active, Clairvoyant Thinking

Building Stones for an Understanding of the Mystery of Golgotha (GA152), lecture of March 7, 1914:
"At the same time as we stand in the midst of the fifth post-Atlantean period, cultivating spiritual science and contributing ever more to the understanding of living thought, of thinking that becomes clairvoyant, we have to prepare for the sixth post-Atlantean period."

Anthroposophical Leading Thoughts (GA26), Letter of August 30, 1924:
"Immeasurably much depends on human ideas not just remaining 'thinking,' but becoming 'seeing' within thinking."

Der Goetheanismus, ein Umwandlungsimpuls und Auferstehungsgedanke. Menschenwissenschaft und Sozialwissenschaft (Goetheanism, a Transformational Impulse and a Resurrection Thought. Human and Social Science) (GA188), lecture of January 5, 1919:
"It is the thinking, not the thoughts, that must become active. This activation of thinking comes from the spiritual world playing into it. And today, if you really begin to think actively, you can hardly do otherwise than allow the spiritual world to play into you."

XIV. The Experience of Thinking

Riddles of Humanity (GA20), Prospects:
"As human beings we can introduce into normal, conscious thinking a stronger development of the will than is present in it during the normal experience of the physical world. In this way, we can move from thinking to *the experience of thinking*. In normal consciousness, we do not experience thinking itself, but rather what we experience through thinking is what is thought. However, there is an inner labor of the soul that gradually brings about one's living not in what is thought, but in the activity of thinking itself."

Das Ewige in der Menschenseele. Unsterblichkeit und Freiheit (The Eternal in the Human Soul. Immortality and Freedom) (GA 67), lecture of February 21, 1918:
"It is a question here of the human being awakening what otherwise is mere combinative (deductive) thinking, which lies at the basis of what is often the only thing considered to be 'science,' of awakening this to inner thinking life. Then thinking becomes a living within thoughts. Then, too, one cannot think about thinking any longer, rather thinking transforms itself into something altogether different. Thinking about thinking transforms itself into a spiritual beholding of thinking."

XV. Wordless Thinking

Rosicrucianism and Modern Initiation (GA 233a), lecture of January 13, 1924:
"And this is how it is with Michael: he strictly rejects and refuses such things as the separative element in human languages. As long as one only encases one's knowledge in

language and does not lift it into thoughts, one cannot come near to Michael. . . . Today one can see a struggle in which Michael strictly rejects and turns back upward-storming ahrimanic spirits, who would like to carry upward what derives from inherited impulses of nationality and which Michael strictly rejects, turns back. . . .

There is in fact the liveliest spiritual battle of this kind going on today because it has become prevalent over a great portion of humanity for there to be no thoughts present, but rather for people to think in words. One only comes to Michael if one comes through the words to true, inner spirit-experiences, if one does not rely on words, but arrives at true inner spirit-experiences. This is in fact the secret of modern initiation: to come out of the word and toward experience of the spiritual."

Kunst und Kunsterkenntnis (Art and Knowledge of Art) (GA271), lecture of May 5, 1918:

"The seer experiences what is for him the content of spiritual experience outside language. This is something difficult to explain since most people think in words, but the seer thinks wordlessly and is then forced to pour what is experienced wordlessly into a language that already has a fixed form. He must accustom himself to the formal relationships of language. He need not feel this as a compulsion, for he enters into the secret of linguistic creativity. He can make himself understood by stripping away the aspect of language that deals in mental pictures. This is why it is so crucial to understand that it is more important *how* the seer says something than *what* he says. What he says is conditioned by the mental picture that everyone brings to it from without. He is forced, in order not to be looked on as a fool, to clothe what he has to say in familiar sentences and representational links. . . . A listener who really understands the seer realizes that the *how* of the expression is what matters; that the seer is careful to formulate one sentence from one standpoint, then to add another from another standpoint.... Therefore it is important to one's understanding to listen less to the mere content—which naturally, as revelation of the world of spirit, is also important—than to penetrate through the content to the way in which the content is expressed, in order to see if the speaker is only combining sentences and theories, or if he is speaking from experience. Speaking out of the world of spirit can be seen in the *how* of what is said—not so much in the content, as far as it has a theoretical character, but in how it comes to expression."

Ibid., lecture of May 6, 1918:
"What is beheld [in the spiritual world] is not beheld in words and does not express itself immediately in words. Therefore, as a seer, one has difficulty in making oneself understood by the outer world since most people think in words, both theoretically and in terms of content, and cannot imagine a life of the soul that goes beyond words. For this reason, one who sensitively experiences the spirit world feels a certain coercion when he has to pour what he experiences into language as it has already been formed. But by silencing what normally lives in language (the capacity for mental images and memory), he can activate for himself the linguistically creative forces themselves, those forces that were active in the evolution of humanity when language first arose. The seer has to place himself in the state of soul whence language first arose; he must develop the double activity of inwardly forming the spiritual thing he beholds and of immersing himself in the spirit of language-formation so that he can unite the one with the other.

Therefore it is important to realize that one must understand the words of the seer differently from other words. When the seer communicates, he has to make use of language, but in such a way that he allows what is active creatively in language to arise again through his emphasizing some things more and others less. . . .

What matters is that he formulates beforehand; what matters is how he says the things, especially things about the spiritual world, not merely what he says. The seer is so hard to understand because all this is so little taken into account, and because when people hear words they remember what the words mean elsewhere."

XVI. The "Two Ways"

In the Afterword to *Knowledge of Higher Worlds and its Attainment* an important step is taken in regard to the view that there are two paths to higher cognitions, one going through *The Philosophy of Freedom* (as an exercise book) and another going through *Knowledge of Higher Worlds*. In the Afterword we read:

" For the supersensible activity of the soul intended here, it is extraordinarily important to understand the experience of pure thinking with complete clarity. For this experience itself is basically already a supersensible activity of the soul. Only it is one through which one does not yet behold anything supersensible. With pure thinking one lives in the supersensible; but this is all one experiences in a supersensible way; one does not yet experience anything else supersensible. Supersensible experience must be a continuation of that soul experience that can already be achieved in the union with pure thinking. For this reason it is so significant to be able to rightly experience this union. For it is from the understanding of this union that the light shines that also brings right insight into the essence of supersensible cognition."

[With this, the two paths are brought into relation to each other, even combined. – G.K.]

XVII. Building Community

Awakening to Community (GA257), lecture of March 3, 1923:
"It is necessary to achieve an understanding of what anthroposophy should be within the Anthroposophical Society: it should be a spiritual path. If it is a spiritual path, then the formation of community will take place."

[If anthroposophy is not grasped and practiced as a spiritual path, then the opposite of community building comes about. – G.K.]

Ibid. lecture of February 28, 1923:
"And if several people come together with what they have from their everyday consciousness, and don't with full sensitivity lift themselves up to the supersensible world, if such people meet together merely to hear the language of the supersensible world in the everyday state of the soul, then there is an infinitely great possibility that they may begin to argue, because in the most natural way they become egotists in relation to each other."

"If people take their normal soul life into their supposed understanding of the teaching from higher worlds, then of course this leads to egotism and argument."

XVIII. Scientificality

Die Verantwortung des Menschen für die Weltentwickelung... (Human Responsibility for World Evolution...) (GA203), lecture of February 8, 1921:
"The work habits in certain orders and in the theosophical movements were not at all applicable to the contents of the anthroposophical movement, because this anthroposophical movement, despite speaking to the heart and soul of every individual person, was at the same time from the start fit to meet all the scientific requirements that can possibly be made in the present time. This last is a fact that has not been taken at all seriously on many sides, even within our membership."

Philosophy, Cosmology, and Religion (GA215), lecture of September 6, 1922:
"Here (in the Goetheanum) a scientific method for the cognition of the supersensible should be developed that is as strict, as exact, as scientific, as the modern scientific method in natural scientific research is supposed to be. One can only attain to the supersensible region if one does not content oneself with the research methods appropriate for what is sensory. Yet one cannot attain to the supersensible worlds scientifically if one operates out of any other spirit than the one that has proved itself so serviceable for the realm of sensory reality."

XIX. The Cultivation of Spiritual Science

In the second of the Eighteen Letters to the Members (*Life, Nature and Cultivation of Anthroposophy*, GA260a) Steiner summarizes his thoughts concerning the cultivation of spiritual science:

"Anthroposophy should be there for people who in their souls seek paths to spiritual experience...

Anthroposophy can only thrive as something living. For the fundamental trait of its being is life. It is life, flowing forth from the spirit. Therefore it needs to be cultivated by the living soul, by the warm heart.

The primal form in which it appears among human beings is the idea; and the first gate it turns to in human beings is insight. If that were not so, it would have no content. It would be mere sentimental feeling. But the true spirit is not sentimental: the language it speaks is clear and content-filled.

But this language is such that it includes not just the intellect but the whole human being. Whoever takes up anthroposophy with the intellect alone kills it by taking it up in this way....

[Anthroposophy] must arise anew each time a human heart turns to a book to learn about it... Only books that can come alive in the reading human being are anthroposophical books.

Anthroposophy can tolerate a book that has taken on a false life in human speech even less than a dead book itself....

Therefore anthroposophy, even when it *has* to live of necessity as literature, can be born anew each time that, in a group of human beings, it seeks the way to their souls in the word. But it will only be born anew where a human being speaks to a fellow human being, not the thoughts one has absorbed."

And from the last letter (ibid., August 10, 1924):
"There is too little awareness ... that anthroposophy should not be grey theory, but true life. True life is the essence of anthroposophy; and if anthroposophy is made into grey theory, then frequently it is by no means a better but a worse theory

than others. Yet anthroposophy only becomes theory if one makes it so, if one kills it. Too little attention is paid to the fact that anthroposophy is not only a different worldview than any other, it *must also be received in a different way*. A person recognizes and experiences the essence of anthroposophy only when he or she receives it in this different way."

XX. Understanding Spiritual Truths

Die Polarität von Dauer und Entwicklung im Menschenleben (The Polarity of Duration and Development in Human Life) (GA184), lecture of September 6, 1918:
"Above all from anthroposophical points of view we must recognize consciously and fundamentally that the knowledge of spiritual things we achieve in the present, no matter how definite, must not be formulated as a sum of absolute dogmas. We have to make it clear to ourselves that others, who will come in the future, will see truer things than we ourselves can see precisely in relation to what we are able to present today. Actually, the spiritual evolution of human beings depends upon this. And every hurdle, every hindrance to the spiritual progress of humanity ultimately depends upon people's not wanting to admit this and wanting instead to have truths transmitted that are not truths of a particular time period, but rather absolute, timeless dogmas.

Kunst- und Lebensfragen im Lichte der Geisteswissenschaft (Questions of Art and Life in the Light of Spiritual Science) (GA162), lecture of June 3, 1915:
"As the spiritual scientists of today stand in regard to the materialists, there will be a small group of people who in the future will go beyond spiritual science to something that, in

this future, will be just as new in relation to spiritual science as spiritual science is new in relation to mere external science. This will put far greater demands on human activity than even spiritual science does."

Notcs

1. R. Steiner, *Spiritual Science as a Foundation for Social Forms* (GA199), lecture of August 20, 1920 (Hudson, NY: Anthroposophic Press, 1986).

2. Cf. G. Kühlewind, *Die Wahrheit Tun* (*Doing the Truth*), chapter entitled "Über das geisteswissenschaftliche Studium" ("On Spiritual Scientific Study") (Stuttgart: Freies Geistesleben, 1982).

3. G. Kühlewind, *Das Licht des Wortes* (*The Light of the Word*), chapter entitled "Das Leben der Bewusstseinsseele" ("The Life of the Consciousness Soul") (Stuttgart: Freies Geistesleben, 1984).

4. D.T. Suzuki, *The Zen Doctrine of No-Mind*, chapter entitled "Seeing into One's Self-Nature" (London: Rider and Company, 1958).

5. G. Kühlewind, *Das Licht des Wortes*, chapter entitled "Das Wortlose Denken" ("Wordless Thinking") (Stuttgart: Freies Geistesleben, 1984).

6. R. Steiner, *The Philosophy of Freedom (Spiritual Activity)* (GA4) (Hudson, NY: Anthroposophic Press, 1986).

7. R. Steiner, *Knowledge of Higher Worlds and Its Attainment* (GA10) (Hudson, NY: Anthroposophic Press, 1986).

8. R. Steiner, *Philosophy, Cosmology, and Religion* (GA215), lecture of September 8, 1922 (Hudson, NY: Anthroposophic Press, 1984); cf. *Inneres Wesen des Menschen und Leben zwischen Tod und neuer Geburt (The Inner Being of Human Beings and Life between Death and a New Birth)* (GA153), lecture of April 10, 1914.

9. R. Steiner, *Die spirituellen Hintergründe der äusseren Welt* (*The Spiritual Background of the Outer World*) (GA177), lecture of October 1, 1917.

10. R. Steiner, *Das christliche Mysterium* (*The Christian Mystery*) (GA97), lecture of February 22, 1907.

11. G. Kühlewind, *Die Diener des Logos* (*Servants of the Logos*), Chapters 9-12; (Stuttgart: Freies Geistesleben, 1981). *Das Licht des Wortes*, op. cit., Chapter 16.

12. R. Steiner, *The Case for Anthroposophy (Riddles of the Soul)* (GA21), Chapter 4, 1 (London: Rudolf Steiner Press, 1970).

13. R. Steiner, *Fruits of Anthroposophy* (GA78), lecture of August 30, 1921 (Hudson, NY: Anthroposophic Press, 1986).

14. R. Steiner, *Community Life, Inner Development, Sexuality and the Spiritual Teacher* (GA253), lecture of October 12, 1915 (Hudson, NY: Anthroposophic Press, 1991).

15. R. Steiner, *Kunst und Kunsterkenntnis* (*Art and Knowledge of Art*) (GA271), lectures of May 5 and 6, 1918.

16. R. Steiner, *The Riddle of Man* (GA20) (Spring Valley, NY: Mercury Press, 1991).

17. See Chapter 1.

18. See Appendix II.

19. R. Steiner, *Initiation, Eternity and the Passing Moment* (GA138), August 28, 1912 (Hudson, NY: Anthroposophic Press, 1980).

20. R. Steiner, *Supersensible Man* (GA231), lecture of November 18, 1923 (London: Anthroposophical Publishing Co., 1961).

21. *The Riddle of Man*, op. cit.

22. *Knowledge of Higher Worlds*, op. cit.

23. See Chapter 6.

24. R. Steiner, *Geographic Medicine* (from *Individuelle Geistwesen und ihr Wirken in der Seele des Menschen*) (GA178), lecture of November 15, 1917 (Spring Valley, NY: Mercury Press, 1986).

25. See ibid., the entire lecture.

26. *The Case for Anthroposophy*, op. cit.

27. G. Kühlewind, *Stages of Consciousness* (Hudson, NY: Lindisfarne Press, 1984).

28. See Appendix XVI.

29. *Spiritual Science as a Foundation for Social Forms*, op cit., lecture of June 8, 1920, see note 1 above. Cf. lecture of August 6, 1920.

30. R. Steiner, *How Can Mankind Find the Christ Again*? (GA187) December 28, 1918 (Hudson, NY: Anthroposophic Press, 1984).

31. See "Foreword" by Jörgen Smit.

Referenccs

Works in German by Rudolf Steiner are cited according to the bibliographic number (GA) of the Collected Works (*Gesamtausgabe*) published by the Rudolf Steiner Verlag, Dornach, Switzerland.

I. WORKS BY RUDOLF STEINER

(GA4) *The Philosophy of Spiritual Activity*. (This work has also been translated under the title *The Philosophy of Freedom*.) Hudson, NY: Anthroposophic Press, 1986.

(GA9) *Theosophy*. Hudson, NY: Anthroposophic Press, 1971.

(GA10) *Knowledge of the Higher Worlds and Its Attainment.* Hudson, NY: Anthroposophic Press, 1986.

(GA13) *An Outline of Occult Science*. Hudson, NY: Anthroposophic Press, 1972.

(GA16/7) *A Road to Self-Knowledge* and *The Threshold of the Spiritual World.* London: Rudolf Steiner Press, 1970.

(GA18) *The Riddles of Philosophy.* Hudson, NY: Anthroposophic Press, 1973.

(GA20) *The Riddle of Man*. Spring Valley, NY: Mercury Press, 1990.

(GA21) *The Case for Anthroposophy [The Riddles of the Soul].* London: Rudolf Steiner Press, 1970.

(GA26) *Anthroposophical Leading Thoughts.* London: Rudolf Steiner Press, 1985.

(GA35) *Philosophy and Anthroposophy* (the title essay of *Philosophie und Anthroposophie*) Spring Valley, NY: Mercury Press, 1988.

(GA55) *Die Erkenntnis des Übersinnlichen in unserer Zeit und deren Bedeutung für das heutige Leben* (13 Vorträge, Berlin und Köln, 1906/7).

(GA56) *Die Erkenntnis der Seele und des Geistes* (15 Vorträge, Berlin und München, 1907/8).

(GA67) *Das Ewige in der Menschenseele. Unsterblichkeit und Freiheit* (10 Vorträge, Berlin, 1918).

(GA78) *Fruits of Anthroposophy* (8 lectures, Stuttgart, 1921). Hudson, NY: Anthroposophic Press, 1986.

(GA84) *Was wollte das Goetheanum und was soll die Anthroposophie?* (11 Vorträge, Basel, Dornach, Prag, Wien, und Paris 1923/24).

(GA95) *At the Gates of Spiritual Science* (14 lectures, Stuttgart, 1906). London: Rudolf Steiner Press, 1986.

(GA97) *Das christliche Mysterium* (31 Vorträge, 1906/7).

(GA99) *Theosophy of the Rosicrucian* (14 lectures, Munich, 1907) London: Rudolf Steiner Press, 1981.

(GA127) *Die Mission der neuen Geistesoffenbarung. Das Christus-Ereignis als Mittelspunktsgeschehen der Erdenevolution* (17 Vorträge, 1911).

(GA137) *Man in the Light of Occultism, Theosophy and Philosophy* (10 lectures, Christiania/Oslo, 1912). London: Rudolf Steiner Press, 1964.

(GA 138) *Initiation, Eternity, and the Passing Moment* (7 lectures, Munich, 1912). Hudson, NY: Anthroposophic Press, 1980.

(GA145) *The Effects of Occult Development on the Self and on the Sheaths of Man* (10 lectures, The Hague, 1913). London: Rudolf Steiner Press, 1979.

(GA152) *Vorstufen zum Mysterium von Golgatha* (10 Vorträge, versch. Städte 1913/14).

(GA154) *The Presence of the Dead* (7 lectures, different cities, 1914). Hudson, NY: Anthroposophic Press, 1990.

(GA159) *Das Geheimnis des Todes. Wesen und Bedeutung Mitteleuropas und die europäischen Volksgeister* (15 Vorträge, versch. Städte, 1915).

(GA162) *Kunst- und Lebensfragen im Lichte des Geisteswissenschaft* (13 Vorträge, Dornach, 1915).

(GA163) *Chance, Providence and Necessity* (8 lectures, Dornach, 1915). Hudson, NY: Anthroposophic Press, 1988.

(GA176) *Aspects of Human Evolution* (8 lectures, Berlin, 1917) and *Karma of Materialism* (9 lectures, Berlin, 1917). Hudson, NY: Anthroposophic Press, 1985 and 1987.

(GA177) *Die spirituellen Hintergründe der äusseren Welt. Der Sturz der Geister der Finsternis)* (14 Vorträge, Dornach, 1917).

(GA178) *Individuelle Geistwesen und ihr Wirken in der Seele des Menschen* (9 Vorträge, St. Gallen, Zürich, Dornach, 1917).

(GA179) *Geschichtliche Notwendigkeit und Freiheit. Schicksalseinwirkungen aus der Welt der Toten* (8 Vorträge, Dornach, 1917).

(GA183) *Die Wissenschaft vom Werden des Menschen* (9 Vorträge, Dornach, 1918).

(GA184) *Die Polarität von Dauer und Entwicklung im Menschenleben. Die kosmische Vorgeschichte der Menschheit)* (15 Vorträge, Dornach, 1918).

(GA186) *Die soziale Grundforderung unserer Zeit. In geänderter Zeitlage* (12 Vorträge, Dornach, 1918).

(GA187) *How Can Mankind Find the Christ Again?* (8 lectures, Dornach and Basel, 1918/19). Hudson, NY: Anthroposophic Press, 1984.

(GA191) *Soziales Verständnis aus geisteswissenschaftlicher Erkenntnis* (15 Vorträge, Dornach, 1919).

(GA193) *Der innere Aspekt des sozialen Rätsels. Luziferische Vergangenheit und ahrimanische Zukunft* (10 Vorträge, versch. Städte, 1919).

(GA196) *Geistige und soziale Wandlungen in der Menschheitsentwickelung* (18 Vorträge, Dornach, 1918).

(GA197) *Polarities in the Evolution of Mankind* (11 lectures, Stuttgart, 1920). London: Rudolf Steiner Press, 1987.

(GA198) *Heilfaktoren für den sozialen Organismus* (17 Vorträge, Dornach und Bern, 1920).

(GA199) *Spiritual Science as a Foundation for Social Forms* (17 lectures, Dornach and Berlin, 1920). Hudson, NY: Anthroposophic Press, 1986.

(GA203) *Die Verantwortung des Menschen für die Weltentwicklung durch seinen geistigen Zusammenhang mit dem Erdplaneten und der Sternenwelt* (18 Vorträge, Stuttgart, Dornach, Den Haag, 1921).

(GA206) *Menschenwerden, Weltenseele und Weltengeist. Erster Teil: Der Mensch als leiblich-seelische Wesenheit in seinem*

Verhältnis zur Welt (13 Vorträge, Stuttgart, Bern, Dornach, 1921).

(GA215) *Philosophy, Cosmology, and Religion* (10 lectures, Dornach, 1922). Hudson, NY: Anthroposophic Press, 1984.

(GA218) *Geistige Zusammenhänge in der Gestaltung des menschlichen Organismus* (16 Vorträge, versch. Städte, 1922).

(GA219) *Man and the World of Stars* (12 lectures, Dornach, 1922). Hudson, NY: Anthroposophic Press, 1963.

(GA220) *Lebendiges Naturerkennen. Intellektueller Sündenfall und spirituelle Sündenerhebung.* (12 Vorträge, Dornach, 1923).

(GA221) *Earthly Knowledge and Heavenly Wisdom* (9 lectures, Dornach, 1923). Hudson, NY: Anthroposophic Press, 1991.

(GA231) *Supersensible Man* (7 lectures, The Hague, 1923). London: Rudolf Steiner Press,1961.

(GA233a) *Rosicrucianism and Modern Initiation* (6 lectures, Dornach, 1924). London: Rudolf Steiner Press, 1982.

(GA237) *Karmic Relationships*, volume III ((11 lectures, Dornach, 1924). London: Rudolf Steiner Press, 1977.

(GA257) *Awakening to Community* (10 lectures, Stuttgart and Dornach, 1923). Hudson, NY: Anthroposophic Press, 1974.

(GA260a) *The Life, Nature and Cultivation of Anthroposophy* (18 articles). London: Rudolf Steiner Press, 1963.

(GA271) *Kunst und Kunsterkenntnis. Grundlagen einer neuen Ästhetik. Das Sinnlich-Übersinnliche in seiner Verwirklichung durch die Kunst* (Essays, 1888, 1909 bis 1921).

(GA316) *Meditative Betrachtungen und Anleitungen zur Vertiefung der Heilkunst* (13 Vorträge, Dornach, 1924).

(GA322) *The Boundaries of Natural Science* (8 lectures, Dornach, 1920). Hudson, NY: Anthroposophic Press, 1983.

(GA324) *The Mathematics Course* (8 lectures, Stuttgart, 1921). Spring Valley, NY: Mercury Press, 1991.

II. BOOKS BY GEORG KÜHLEWIND

Die Wahrheit Tun. Stuttgart: Verlag Freies Geistesleben, 1982.
Das Licht des Wortes. Stuttgart: Verlag Freies Geistesleben, 1984.
Die Diener des Wortes. Stuttgart: Verlag Freies Geistesleben,1981.
Stages of Consciousness. Hudson: Lindisfarne Press, 1984.